unity.

unity.

A tapestry of story to spark belonging, connection and liberation

curated by
NATASHA GILMOUR & VARI McKECHNIE

First published by the kind press 2023

Compilation copyright © the kind press 2023
"Ethereal touch" copyright © by Rayne Jobling-Paitai
"Rich on the inside" copyright © by Tara Winters
"The mid-life sensual awakening" copyright © by Sonia Bavistock
"The first year" copyright © by Hannah Thomas
"Embracing the power of internal safety" copyright © by Kate Jones
"We're more similar than we're different, especially us women" copyright © by Tammy Guest
"Awake" copyright © by Natalie Simes
"A timeless love story" copyright © by Pina DiDonato
"Dating in the modern world" copyright © by Suzie de Jonge
"The golden ticket south" copyright © by Ana Asanovic
"Happily ever after" copyright © by Anita Carr

Typesetting by Nicola Matthews, Nikki Jane Design
Cover design by Vari McKechnie

The moral right of the authors to be identified as the author of this work has been asserted.

All rights reserved. Without limiting the rights under copyright reserved above, no part of this publication may be reproduced, stored in or introduced into a retrieval system, or transmitted, in any form or by any means (electronic, mechanical, photocopying, recording or otherwise) without the prior written permission of the publisher of this book.

A catalogue record for this book is available from the National Library of Australia.

Trade Paperback ISBN: 978-0-6458656-5-3
eBook ISBN: 978-0-6458656-6-0

The kind press acknowledges Australia's First Nations peoples as the traditional owners and custodians of this country, and we pay our respects to their elders, past and present.

THE
KIND
PRESS

www.thekindpress.com

To the women, past, present and future, whose thread of story is woven into the tapestry of life. Our stories matter and help to illuminate the world.

Threads

Introduction vi

Chapter 1
ETHEREAL TOUCH
Rayne Jobling-Paitai
1

Chapter 2
RICH ON THE INSIDE
Tara Winters
17

Chapter 3
THE MID-LIFE SENSUAL AWAKENING
Sonia Bavistock
37

Chapter 4
THE FIRST YEAR
Hannah Thomas
53

Chapter 5
EMBRACING THE POWER OF INTERNAL SAFETY
Kate Jones
69

Chapter 6
WE'RE MORE SIMILAR THAN WE'RE DIFFERENT, ESPECIALLY US WOMEN
Tammy Guest
89

Chapter 7
AWAKE
Natalie Simes
103

Chapter 8
A TIMELESS LOVE STORY
Pina DiDonato
117

Chapter 9
DATING IN THE MODERN WORLD
Suzie de Jonge
131

Chapter 10
THE GOLDEN TICKET SOUTH
Ana Asanovic
147

Chapter 11
HAPPILY EVER AFTER: A WORK IN PROGRESS
Anita Carr
168

Final thoughts 177

Introduction

To the fearless souls among us, the vanguards of our time, this is your clarion call. It beckons the audacious, the relentless, the visionaries and the believers to chart a course toward stories that set ablaze the spirits of belonging, connection and liberation.

In a world sometimes fractured and disjointed, we are the architects of Unity. Stories are our tools, weaving the intricate fabric of our shared human experience, transcending the constraints of time and space. Know this: within life's rich tapestry, each woman's story gleams as a golden thread, embodying her resilience, wisdom and the vast expanse of her heart.

This book not only pays tribute to the women who walked this path before us, but acknowledges that their narratives laid the foundation upon which we build today. As you journey through these pages and explore the lives, dreams and triumphs of women, remember this truth: you are never alone. Your story is not an echo but a vital strand in the tapestry of humanity. Let the stories within these pages not just inspire you but inspire you to seize your role, seek out the stories that resonate with your essence and boldly share your narrative with the world. May it kindle a fire in your soul, spark a flame that burns brightly with the understanding that you are a pivotal part of an expansive web of stories—each one unique, each one resplendent, all contributing to a world steeped in greater kindness and introspection. Your quest for truth has unveiled a profound revelation: every woman's story mirrors your own, and together, they crescendo into a symphony of voices.

May you discover deep belonging in the shared experiences of the women in these stories. May you forge connections that transcend boundaries, empower you to stand tall, and illuminate your uniqueness. Let this book serve as a resolute call to action, a declaration that courage is the path to a future where generations of women will be inspired by our audacity and empowered to take their own bold strides. The time for action is now. Rise, embrace the call, and let our stories light the way for the women of tomorrow.

Chapter 1

Ethereal Touch

Rayne Jobling-Paitai

To the guardian of flowers and all the women who nurtured me. From seed to seedling, to flower we grow.

There is a garden I visit every now and then. In this garden there is a woman—she is the guardian of flowers.

I have seen her plant and grow the most beautiful flowers, their stems strong and roots grounded; their petals bright when the light is right. I have seen her nurture the soil beneath their feet and feed the growing life with goodness and love, protection and wisdom. She is a grower in a sea of reapers, she is a nurturer in a mass of neglect, she sees the ladybird beneath the leaf because she stops to look at the leaf. Her steps never crush hidden treasures because those treasures never hide from her.

This is the woman I visit in the garden, and this is what she taught me.

*

I went to see her the other day, only this time she wasn't there. Her sole watering can, bright yellow against the muddy ground, sits unaccompanied by the archway entrance. The garden is no small venture, it stretches over hills and through gullies, towering trees providing a quenching shade for plants and little creatures alike. I wander through the pebble covered walkways, littered with wayward sprouts opposing the intended refinement of a clear path. There are no fences, there are no boundaries. It is so open you feel as though you are experiencing the world all at once and for the very first time. There are flowers everywhere, in every shape, colour, form, height and size; she doesn't discriminate. I keep winding and weaving through a jungle of life, potted flower beds and bramble bushes akin. I quickly realise I am lost. In an ocean of colour, there is no consistency to hold on to. Everywhere I look more and more flowers appear. Without her guidance it is overwhelming. How can one singular person care for so many things? I imagine her little yellow watering can out of breath with exasperation, droplets dribbling from its spout in a pant.

I wander and wander until the bushes start thinning out, the speckled sunlight becoming full rays. The path begins to clear, there are no longer misbehaving sprouts upsetting the walkway. A rope boundary appears, softly nudging the larger leaves and plants back into alignment. I trace the rope with my hand, letting it guide me. I pass a sprinkler system that darts off down every path and covers the rows of flower beds ahead of me. I guess there was only so much a little yellow watering can could do. I look back over my shoulder, to the lawless spread of nature behind me and while I do see wild beauty, I also see angst and unrest. Ahead of me, there is an arrow pointing back towards the entrance. It is the only sign I've seen so far, so I hurry along.

As I reach the entry again, I see her standing at the top of the hill overlooking the garden. I walk up to meet her. Standing next to her, the top of her head reaches just under my chin. She doesn't acknowledge me yet, but from here I can see her whole garden. Her yellow watering can, small as the pollen centre of a flower, the delightful chaos scattered throughout the early parts of the garden and the spiral centre that draws all paths inwards—the hearth. While some parts are trimmed and maintained, others need little to no maintenance. There are even instances where you can see she has tried to sculpt something, just to have it rebel and twist the opposite way; suffocating the plant next to it.

I've never seen her garden from here before.

Feeling confused by her silence, I observe her face. Her eyes are closed, her chin tilted up, breath falling out of her nose in deep exhales. Then her eyes open; a light-eyed entity of goodness, with eyes of fluorite green, like sea-soaked glass, rounded and softened to withstand the push and pull of life. She has the eyes of a feline warrior, bright and fierce, speckled with flakes of golden amber—warm for those she loves. When you meet a gaze of such intensity, your vulnerabilities become pillars of strength. And your weaknesses are nurtured, watered and coaxed to shed their shell. You are raw and absolute and wholly you in the moment she meets your eyes.

There are no words spoken, only felt. She tells me that, 'every time you give, you give a piece of yourself. And there are only so many times you can do that before you run out of thread'. She describes it like a tapestry of life. Woven and fused, pulled and pinched in some areas, while detailed and intricate in others and some simply mundane. This is the unity of living. It is not always constant, there is no consistency, there is only dynamical being. And maybe that's the irony—that life *is* consistently dynamic. She gestures to her garden and tells me its story in silence. How it replicates the expression of empathy, the act of giving for the growth and benefit of others.

I see the garden with clearer eyes. The chaotic front of the garden cannot be tamed because she began growing it too quickly. She spread too many seeds, and gave too much all at once and draining herself dry. How can one yellow watering can feed an entire field of hungry flowers? It can't. There are some empty spaces as you move further along—spaces she chose to leave empty. There are some plants that grow taller than others, shading the smaller in their wake; she let them be. Even further along, I can see the purpose of the sprinkler system now. Wound around the last parts of the garden, sending light mists to cool every leaf it can touch, attending to those she couldn't stretch herself to. She takes my hand, and I can hear her heart sing.

We walk back down the hill to the entrance of the garden. She's heading for the watering can. I move to grasp it first, trying to initiate a helping hand. She stops me before I can latch onto the fluorescent handle. She sets it aside and links her arm with mine. Together we take a walk through the garden, mud splashing up the sides of our welly boots. We pass a sunflower, its petals dull and head drooped to the side. She moves forward and peels back the leaves sheltering its path to the sun. Its small narrow petals twitch with warmth and, arching towards the rays, it blooms.

*

Empathy is a cruel curse and an angelic blessing. Like everything that works in contradiction, empathy is no exception. Givers learn to take, and takers learn to give—an ouroboros of compassion. It's a hard, lifelong lesson people everywhere struggle with and battle against. It exhausts, it haunts, it injures, it depletes. But it also teaches, guides, strengthens and praises.

Your compassion is vital. It is the heart line that shapes your hand. It is the sweetener to your tea, a single sugar cube of goodness. But compassion burns as quickly as dry kindling to a starved fire. For some, the act of giving is reward enough, but that reward will not sustain them. For others, it is the assembly of merit, an invaluable bank of kind gestures and warm regards—a credit system.

There is no shame in wanting praise or recognition for your actions. There is no judgment in wanting kindness in return when all you do is give and give and give. Be selfish with your desires, because only you know how to ask for them. So, ask. Give because you want to give and take when you need to take. The day will grow older, and the time will wind faster, but your heart will only ever beat in sync with you, so listen to it.

There is a girl I know who wrote me letters in high school. They were always A4 lined pages, torn out of her exercise book before the bell rang for the end of class. Every line was full, front and back, and heavy with words. Scratched into the paper with a black ballpoint pen, sometimes blue, she would write to me. Her alphabet was so close together, like the letters were hugging. I found the letters recently. Folded four times over, hidden in between pages of old journals, scrap bits of paper stuffed into overflowing folders of forgotten keepsakes. One after the other, I read and re-read every line. She never spoke the way she wrote, which is why I cherished them so much. She used sarcasm and humour to show she cared but her written words meant the world to me. Her kindness was never weighted, her compassion always true and her friendship forever treasured.

When you find people who add value to your day just by being a part of it, hold on to them. And if they drift, like a piece of bark afloat in a swirling sea of tumultuous life, let them drift. They are choosing to swim with their own tide, to reach a different horizon—let them. But don't forget, tides have a funny way of bringing back what belongs on land.

Be patient.

However, there are those who use this compassionate gift as a source of sustenance, relying on its nutrition for everyday survival. This is where your thread runs thin, threatening to snap. When receiving becomes expected, rather than appreciated. A lot of the time they don't realise what they are taking from you, until they have nothing more to take. So weave the safety nets and cushion the falls but remember to move your finger before tying the final bow. There have been many people I've tried to hold, so many bows I've tied, so many times I lay twisted in the thread from my own wheel, my spindle empty. The process of detangling is messy, frustrating and draining.

We often forget ourselves in dire situations. Whether it be about us or not, we forget to give ourselves a minute to catch up. Have you ever been listening to yourself give great and sound advice to someone and think, are you practising what you're preaching? I can assure you, you aren't. It is easier to be kind to others than it is to be kind to yourself, plain and simple. So, when you feel your thread pull tight, loosen your grip because something is trying to protect you.

But what do you do when your thread is cut prematurely? What do you do when you have more to give, but your soft yarn is met with scissors? No one prepares you for rejection, when all you have ever associated with love, kindness and compassion, is acceptance.

And the one holding the scissors is usually the one who can see your *ethereal touch* …

*

When calamity comes knocking down doors of blissful ignorance, it is met with crumbling devastation. It doesn't need a key or permission to enter. It doesn't wipe its feet on the welcome mat, because it is not welcome. The shoes it wears are heavy and loud, crusted with mud, trailing tears of splatted dirt onto newly laid carpet.

An unwanted visitor; cold in a house of warmth.

I often question place as character and the role it plays when tragedy occurs. There is a feeling of discomfort when you realise you have no control over your surroundings when calamity comes knocking. Nevertheless, calamity did in fact come knocking, but not on my door.

You've met the woman in the garden; she lives in the pages behind you. Well, calamity took a stroll through her garden and didn't want to leave. Standing before her sanctuary, the beautifully woven archway lay blackened with soot, scratched from something sharp and intrusive. The grooves it made were deep marks that would scar. I ducked my head and made my way through. Splotches of black marked rose petals and stained lilies, coated vines and dug up roots. I kept going. I found myself drawn towards the centre, the hearth of her garden.

As I got closer, a man appeared at my side, a few dew drops clung to the fabric of the hat he wore. Through the warmth of his chestnut eyes lay a sadness, new and heavy. We didn't speak. He only walked ahead of me, guiding me forward—he knew the way. A moment later, a woman to my right took my hand in hers. Her pale blue eyes shone against a skin of English snow, glowing and radiant, with dark curly hair that matched my own. We smiled at each other, but it didn't reach our eyes. We continued walking. To my left now was another woman. I had to look down to meet her gaze. Under a bob of reddish hair that matched the blush on her cheeks, I saw her fragile skin creasing her brow that was pulled tight with worry. I took her cool hand in mine and squeezed it, her bangles chiming as they clinked together in time with our step.

We reached the centre. There she was, sat on a chair tilted against the grain of the bricks that lay rockily beneath her feet. She was a sunflower; her face chasing the early morning rays— basking. The chair was bathed in a cool yellow light, warming as the day grew older. A slice of contrast to the shady surrounds that envelope the garden, bushy with wet shrubbery, laid thick over a mossy underlay. She sat with her back to our faces that were gaunt and long with worry. Her back so straight, beneath the knitted wool of her cardigan, her spine was like glass. Her chin tilted up, her hands softly cradled a cup of hot water, clouded with brewing ginger root. The steam spiralled upwards, warming her chin, drifting around her face and swirling into the cold air around her. Her light green eyes were closed, her brow smooth, nothing doused in tension; nothing we could see. But we knew what lay beneath. Calamity spreads like a poison in her body, we knew it was there, she knew it was there, but it knew we wanted it out.

One day, I will paint what I am about to describe to you. The way bodies fall into embrace is one of the most influential art forms one can witness. It involves seeing the grasp of hands creasing clothing or smoothing skin, it is the way breath falls in synchronicity, it is the way cold is perceived and warmth is received. Artists of centuries past have sculpted, painted, woven and pressed its magnitude into history over and over.

Is there a person in your life you think of when I describe the feeling of an embrace? It could be a mother's cradle, a lover's caress, a father's cuddle. Or it could be none of those. I want to render a picture in your mind, as clear as the resin I will use to preserve it in mine.

This is the embrace I know.

We wrapped around her like a blanket of woven tapestry, each of us holding a space for her in a way that was so different yet extremely alike. A mother and a daughter, a sister and a sister, a husband and a wife, a niece and an aunty. We made a circle around her. We watered the garden around her with fresh winter tears. In our circle of embrace, she held her hand out to me and I grasped it with two. I could always feel her, always sense her, she had a way of reaching others with an invisible touch only some could sense. Only this time she told me to stop reaching for her as I felt her retract away, like a fern coiling in on itself. I was confused and scared.

Why was she pulling back? Doesn't she realise the reason we are all here? Every one of us cares, every one of us can hold her—we can hold her.

The brown-eyed man smiled one of those tight-lipped smiles, conveying a sense of understanding I still couldn't quite grasp. And then I felt it, as crisp as the snap of a snow pea popping in your mouth, only this one wasn't sweet. It was cold. It was silence. When all I wanted to hear was her song. It was like the wind changed its heading and was billowing towards her in all directions, like she was drawing in a breath from the world. The hum of energy around her was electric.

She had spent her whole life giving and now she was asking for some back, only she wouldn't take it from me. My thread was severed, the ends lay frayed and fizzled. I tried to mend the break, tried to conjure more thread but nothing was working. I was indescribably frustrated, it bubbled past my lips in a silent wail. Her sea glass, green eyes met mine and I felt the weight of her action, the reason for her withdrawal.

She was protecting her tulip in preparation for a long winter.

The woman in the garden held her family; but they held her back just that little bit tighter. She was worried for the garden, for the health of the flowers. We each brought out a watering can, one brown, one blue, one red and one green, and began watering.

*

Now you know the woman in the garden and have witnessed the lessons she has taught. You know how she feeds the soil of those around her, you know how she waters their leaves and tends to their needs, but now you also know that the soil around her is blackened with calamity. A sunflower's pine for a warmer day, in the midst of the harshest winter she'll ever know. She has learnt to call in favours of kindness past, though she doesn't need to call, they are already here.

You each have a place where you grow, where you turn stone to diamond. Find that place and understand its intricacies, listen and learn, watch and nurture and your blossoms will bloom. Friction is OK, confusion is allowed, there is no formula, only trial. But stick around long enough to witness the error and watch it fester. Trim the extra length, and then weave some more.

Protect those in need of protection but remember to reach for others when you get stuck. Keep tying those bows, keep watering those flowers and keep spinning that wheel, but remember in those moments when you feel your thread's fragility begin to unravel, loosen your hold and wind it back in.

About the author

Rayne Jobling-Paitai

Rayne Jobling-Paitai is a writer, illustrator and self-publisher who contributes to the creative arts world through her lyrical writing and authentic drawings. Rayne has illustrated and curated three children's books in the last year as well as launching her personal blog, The Tulip Row Diaries, all whilst completing her Bachelor of Creative Writing. Her contributing chapter to Unity is her first experience as a published author and a significant milestone on her journey to becoming an established writer.

@rjpillustations_
www.thetuliprowdiaries.site

Chapter 2

Rich on the inside

Tara Winters

To my beautiful children who are my greatest teachers, my husband who saw the real me from the very beginning and my parents upon whose shoulders I so gratefully stand.

It was a flippant question, and one intended as a compliment, but it was a question that would eventually shake the foundations upon which I had built my life.

I was twenty-nine years old and working in the London office of a global investment bank. From the outside, it looked like I had cracked the code for success. I was happily married, we'd bought and renovated our first home, had our first baby, I was earning big money and with a solid track record of being a high achiever, I was only just getting started.

While on maternity leave, I came across a book that detailed a long list of behaviours that women should either stop or start doing in order to be taken more seriously in the corporate world. At a time when I was feeling nervous about my impending return to work and how I would juggle being brilliant at both mothering and full-time corporate accounting, it captured my attention. There were tips on what to wear, what to say and which strategic moves to make to get noticed. It was like being handed a secret manifesto on how to win the corporate game. I decided to put it into practice as a sort of social experiment and see if it worked.

A month later, a re-invented version of me walked back

through the big glass doors and into my first day in the office. Gone were the flowing skirts and dangling earrings I had worn previously. In came the androgynous monochrome pant suits, the pin-striped shirts, the pointy stilettos and the slicked back ponytail. I began answering my phone in a direct and far less friendly tone, saying only my first and last names rather than the friendly 'Hello, Tara speaking!' I had used previously. I pretended I hadn't recently become a mother to a small human being. I didn't put a single photo of my son on my desk and I rarely mentioned, or even alluded to, the fact I was now a mother. I logged on from home late at night after he fell asleep and on the occasional weekend to prove my commitment. My work was of the same high standard it had always been, but I now drew attention to it by sending weekly emails highlighting my successes. And, in my biggest move of all, I requested a meeting with my boss's boss to let her know I wanted to be promoted to Vice President level and to ask her advice on how to get there.

I didn't know it at the time, but that meeting was about to blow up my life.

The meeting itself was an incredible success, just as the book had predicted it would be. As I was leaving her office, my boss's boss stopped me and said, 'You know, Tara, ever since you've come back from maternity leave, you've seemed like a totally different person. You're on fire. You look amazing. Who even are you?'

I laughed, thanked her again, and walked out of her office. And in what should have been a moment of self-congratulation, one question echoed louder and louder in my mind as I pressed the button for the elevator: *who even are you?*

In the following weeks and months, the question continued to bounce around my mind without any answers, and the exhaustion of trying to maintain my success against the backdrop of new motherhood began to set in. I started to feel like a sleep-deprived sprint runner, racing my way through all the things I needed to do every day and then collapsing in bed before having to wake up and do it all again only a few hours later.

The gloss of the corporate world began to diminish my spirit. It was getting harder and harder to pretend to be someone I wasn't. The social experiment was absolutely working, but I was wearing clothes that didn't feel like me, filtering my personality out of everything and stripping any emotion from my conversations in order to be seen as highly professional. I was covering up the hot mess of new motherhood to appear like I had it all together, and I was growing increasingly homesick for the blue skies and family support I had left back in Sydney.

One Monday afternoon, I was feeling more bone-tired than usual and wondered when all my hard work would finally pay off so I could relax and know that I had "made it". I took a rare moment to pause and look out across the sprawling office floor with all its desks, computers and highly successful humans. It suddenly dawned on me that, in spite of their enormous salaries and staggeringly huge bonuses, not one of those humans struck me as being particularly happy.

The trajectory I was on, and that I had been on for my entire life up until that point, came into sharp focus. I was thirty, pregnant with our second baby, about to be promoted to Vice President level and had everything I was told would make me happy. It all looked good on the outside but, aside from my beautiful and growing family, it didn't feel good on the inside.

For the first time ever, I had no idea what I was doing with my life and where I was headed. All I knew was that I felt really, really lost.

The following few years were a frenetic and jumbled haze of resigning, moving back to Sydney, giving birth to our second and third babies and maintaining my corporate career as best I could. With endless nappies to be changed and middle-of-the-night feeds and cuddles to be had, there was no time to ponder my state of being lost or to figure out who I was. And truthfully? Part of me was thankful for the distraction from those bigger questions that had quietly begun to gnaw at me.

Besides, motherhood brought with it its own set of questions. My body, my career, my freedom and my ability to get out of the house without a two-hour military-style operation had all fallen by the wayside. All the things I thought made me "me" had changed. My "good girl" tendencies had graduated into an all-encompassing mission to be a "good mother" and with my youngest baby having chronic health issues that needed a lot of managing, my perfectionism went into overdrive. I was exhausted. I felt like I was failing and I didn't know how to ask for help. After all, I was the high achiever who believed I could handle everything.

For someone who has always had control of their life, or

the illusion of control at least, it was a humbling experience to realise I had none. The only way I could manage in that season of my life was to surrender any idea of control and take one day, and sometimes just one hour, at a time. In that state of surrender, I felt myself being drawn to a local yoga class for what I thought would be some gentle exercise and relaxation. Looking back now, that yoga class was, in fact, my re-entry point into a magical world I had forgotten years earlier in my rush to be a "normal" and successful adult.

Having grown up in 1980s Australia as the child of Indian immigrants, I had never really felt a sense of belonging. Subtle and not-so-subtle messaging received throughout my childhood and teenage years let me know that my brown skin marked me as different and weird. As a result, I'd spent many years doing everything I could to fit in, be a people pleaser and a good girl so as not to "other" myself any further.

I was fascinated by my grandfather, an astrologist and palm reader. I loved the smell of incense that sometimes wafted from my mother's Hindu altar. But these mystical and spiritual leanings were closely associated with my "otherness". And when, as a young adult, my conversations about mystical things were laughed at or belittled by others, I quickly learned it was easier to just assimilate and be normal.

So, it was refreshing to be in this beautiful yoga community and back in an environment where I could have conversations about things like manifesting after years of being immersed in the logic-dominated world of corporate finance. I still kept my two worlds very separate, but life started to take on a magical and spiritual quality once again. My yoga teacher did energy healings too, so I followed the nudge and found myself sitting in her yoga studio one evening, eyes closed and feeling a little out of my comfort zone.

'You're really attached to the idea of hard work!' she exclaimed after a few minutes. I was a little confused. I was a hard worker, yes, but I thought that was just a normal part of adult life.

Didn't everyone work hard?

'Well, yeah, working hard has got me to where I am today,' I replied.

'Are you sure about that?'

'Yes, I'm sure.'

'So, you're saying that all the best things that have happened in your life are because you worked hard?'

When she put it that way, I wasn't so sure. My mind became a stream of one example after another of beautiful things in my life that I hadn't had to work for. There was the serendipity of meeting the love of my life on my last night in town. The job transfer to London, a dream come true, offered to me by a senior executive who hadn't known that I'd resigned from the company the day before to go travelling and live in London. There were our three beautiful children, even though I had been told at the age of fifteen that it was unlikely I would ever be able to conceive children without medical intervention. When I really thought about it, there was a lot of good fortune, serendipitous meetings and out of the blue opportunities.

It was then I started to think that maybe I didn't have to

rely *only* on hard work to create a life I loved; that maybe there was room for magic too, big magic that I couldn't quite fathom with my human mind. The belief I had held onto for years after watching my immigrant parents work incredibly hard for money—that I too, would have to work really hard to feel financially secure, let alone abundant—slowly began to unwind and my brain started to open up to other possibilities.

That was when my manifesting adventure took off. By releasing the old stories I carried around money and aligning my energy and actions to create more abundance, it felt like a secret key had turned inside a hidden lock. Money and other forms of abundance started to find their way to me in strange and wonderful ways. An insurance company sent me a letter along with a cheque for a few hundred dollars, saying they had miscalculated my premiums five years ago. Holiday accommodation bookings would have various issues crop up at the last minute, leading to free upgrades. I'd receive unexpected discounts on things I was about to pay full price for. And while the amounts were small to begin with, I was incredibly grateful for them because to me, they were evidence I didn't have to work hard for an abundant life and they signalled a connection to something big and wondrous.

After dipping my toe back into the mystical world, old memories surfaced from my late teens and early twenties when I would often seek the counsel of tarot readers, many of whom told me I was "a healer" or that I had "healing hands". All these years later, I felt drawn to the tarot again and one day I had the impulse to dust off the tarot cards my husband had bought for me in London a decade earlier.

I started to do readings for myself and for a few friends. We often found ourselves sitting wide-eyed at the truth and wisdom coming through. And then one day, my son brought home a note from school that had my body tingling and my intuition going into overdrive. It was asking for market stall holders for a "ladies" fundraiser event being held at the school.

I kept getting a strong feeling that I should run a tarot reading stall, which seemed ridiculous because I wasn't qualified enough to charge people for readings. I was terrified of "outing" myself as a spiritual weirdo to all the other school mums in our conservative suburban area, and the corporate high achiever in me felt embarrassed about what people might think of me running a market stall.

The strong feeling didn't go away and my husband, who has always supported me to follow my heart, encouraged me to be brave and sign up. In spite of my nerves, every single reading was a joy for me. I felt connected to the beautiful human in front of me, as well as to something bigger than the both of us. Far from being tiring, doing back-to-back readings for four hours energised me and I was sorry to have to turn people away at the end of the night when the event finished. I was in awe of how the cards had resonated with complete strangers and sparked deep conversations about their inner worlds. And there were so many commonalities between the women that I wished I could bring them together to talk as a group so they knew they weren't alone in what they were experiencing. It was a profound experience for me, and one that would later inspire me to find a way to continue doing this kind of work.

But until I could work out how to do that, I continued treading water as a working mother. Then, within the space of six months, three of the people closest to me, my husband, mother and a dear friend all received confronting medical diagnoses. Thankfully, each of them, as one doctor put it, "dodged a bullet" and went on to receive a clean bill of health, but it was a very challenging time. It threw me into a deep spiritual awakening where I began to come to terms with the fragility and the gift of life and how I'd been semi-sleepwalking through much of mine.

Far from being a pretty picture of spiritual bliss, it was a messy and imperfect process of trying to sort through how I'd arrived at where I was and which pieces I wanted to take with me as I travelled to wherever I was going next. In truth, it felt like a breaking apart and a questioning of everything, including myself. Most of the time, it felt raw and vulnerable and there were a lot of unprocessed emotions I had to work through.

One thing that made everything feel a bit lighter was a family trip to Bali to attend my cousin's wedding. Being a meticulous planner, I had every detail of our trip organised ahead of time, including the outfits our kids would wear as part of the bridal party. One night, a couple of weeks before we were due to fly to Bali, I was driving home from dinner with friends when out of nowhere, I heard a voice in my head. It felt like a thought, only I hadn't generated it. It was more like I had *received* it. The voice said, 'check the kids' passports.' I immediately dismissed it, assuming it was my perfectionist mind overthinking as usual. Besides, I was sure I had already checked the kids' passports months ago. Then I heard the thought-voice again, this time more insistent, repeating, 'check the kids' passports.' When I got home, I checked the kids' passports, just to be sure. I was astonished to see that two of them had expired. Thankfully, I was able to get them renewed in the nick of time, saving us from being turned away at the airport and missing my cousin's wedding. Looking back, that was the first time I heard my spirit guide talking to me.

Back home from Bali, and still in the midst of a spiritual awakening, I was on the lookout for signs to show me the way towards a more fulfilling life. One evening, while out for a walk in my local neighbourhood, the sign arrived in the form of a podcast episode featuring a guest interview with the founder of a life coaching academy. Listening to her speak made time stand still and gave me full body goosebumps. I stopped walking and as the sun was setting to my right, I took out my phone and looked up their website. Everything about it felt like home.

It is no understatement to say that the life coaching course changed my life. It gave me the tools, the self-awareness and the confidence to do something I had been doing naturally for most of my life. At a time when I felt nervous about being the black sheep amongst my family and friends for doing something so different, it also gave me a community of like-minded people.

A few months after the course finished, I resigned from my

accounting job so I could focus on building my life coaching practice. At first, the freedom was exhilarating. It felt so good to finally be free of the corporate world and to do work that felt meaningful and connected to who I really was.

It didn't take long, however, for me to start questioning myself. With the stable and sizeable pay cheques of the corporate world gone, a feeling of insecurity crept up on me. It takes time to build a business and without the validation of dollars streaming in, I started to doubt my value and worthiness. Logically speaking, our family was fine financially and had nothing to worry about. But the way we behave around money isn't logical. The way we grow up around money impacts us deeply and its effects can linger on for a lifetime unless you do the inner work.

I had grown up with a deep insecurity around money. My parents had immigrated to Australia with very little money in their pockets, no jobs, two small kids and no safety net. I grew up feeling insecure about money and associating it with survival. When you've got that operating system running in the background of your brain, no amount of money will ever be enough to feel secure. With very little money coming in from my fledgling business, my sense of self was shaken up yet again and I found myself experiencing a dark night of the soul.

With that one last piece of my identity stripped away, I was finally able to sit with the question of: *who am I?* If I'm not my achievements, my title at work, the roles I play in my personal life, the amount of money I make or my physical appearance, then who am I?

I think most of us are scared to ask that question because we're afraid the answer is "I'm a nobody". In a society that teaches us to value ourselves and others on these things, we're frightened we might have no value without them. That's why it feels like such a hard knock when we lose a job, retire, have a baby, become an empty nester, our bodies age or change, relationships end, the stock market falls or our business flounders. It feels like a loss of identity and the first step on a slippery slope to becoming a "nobody".

Having travelled through that dark night of the soul and out the other side, I have come to believe it's quite the opposite. The beauty and value of who we are resides *beneath* all these things. When we learn to connect with and love our inner self, our true essence, even with all its shadows and dark sides, we experience a level of inner security and freedom that never falters. It helps us to ride the inevitable waves and changes of life with so much more grace and self-compassion. And we start to recognise and feel connected to the exquisite beauty and inherent value of the people all around us.

Once I detached my sense of self from the amount of money I was making, the money started flowing in quite easefully and I began to manifest increasingly large amounts. Around this time, the world economy started to feel unsettled and with rising interest rates, inflation and energy prices, a lot of people started to feel unsettled too. With my now heightened intuition and lifelong sensitivity, I could feel the fear and heaviness of the collective and I felt called to help. I knew a thing or two about money in both the practical and mystical sense, and I wanted to be of service. One day, in meditation, I had a one-sided conversation with whichever higher power was listening. I said, 'I'm here to serve. Tell me what to do, and I'll do it. I just need to know that my needs will be taken care of.' Two days later, I received an answer. It was an unexpected cheque for a six-figure amount.

Keen to fulfil my end of the agreement, I started sharing my thoughts around money more widely on social media, including the "weirder" and more mystical elements. It felt edgy for me to show these sides of myself so publicly when, for years, I had run in the other direction from anything that might make me stand out as being different. Coming out of the spiritual closet can leave a person feeling vulnerable and open to judgement, and because I'd already been "othered" as a young person for being brown-skinned, that felt doubly true for me.

In truth, things had also started to get a whole lot weirder. I was connecting with that thought-voice more often through meditation and journalling. One day, I heard the thought-voice tell me its name: Ezra. Never having heard that name before, I Googled it and discovered Ezra is a Hebrew name that means "help" or "helper".

Now I felt *really* weird. And really alone. It's a big leap to go from twenty years of corporate accounting to being a money and spirituality coach who channels a helpful spirit guide called Ezra. I didn't talk about this with many people. I was unsure of how to approach and integrate this into my work and life.

Thankfully, divine help was sent in the form of Marianne Williamson, a world-renowned spiritual teacher, who happened to be doing a speaking tour. At her event, Marianne spoke about the concept of each of us having a divine assignment. Whatever body, whatever circumstances, whatever life we find ourselves in, that is our divine assignment. Listening to her, a huge realisation dropped in for me: all those things I had seen as my crosses to bear were actually my divine assignment. All those things that made me feel weird, alone, unable to fit in—they had a purpose.

My internal clash between my eastern heritage and western upbringing, my affinity with both money and spirituality, my desire to be a deeply present mother as well as have a wider impact in this world ... they were all planted within me for a reason. It was up to me to find a way to integrate these dualities within myself and to collect and heal the aspects of me I had discarded in my desperation to fit in. And in creating the bridge and the medicine within myself, I would be able to share it with others.

The unexpected gift in all of this was that in leaning into my weirdness and stepping into being more me, I began meeting more people who felt like home. In discovering who I really was and taking off all the masks I had learned to wear, I began to radiate a truer, more authentic version of myself. I wasn't for everyone and that was something I had to make peace with. But in cultivating an inner sense of belonging and acceptance for myself, I began to magnetise people who I could be myself with and with whom I could find acceptance and belonging.

I now have an answer to the question that upended my life almost fifteen years ago. Who am I? I'm a mystic, an old soul, a starseed. A lover of beauty, truth, humanity and love. A believer in kindness and connection and a fulfiller of divine assignments. And I know that whatever I'm looking for on the outside—love, acceptance, belonging, connection, security or richness—must first start on the inside and radiate out from there.

About the author

Tara Winters

Tara Winters is an award-winning money coach, soul guide, speaker, writer and mother of three. After decades of hiding her spirituality while working as a corporate accountant and downplaying her money wisdom in the spiritual world, she discovered that money and spirituality can, in fact, truly elevate one another.

She now brings her unique medicine to lovingly guide you back to your soul and to radically shift the way you see, relate to and create money so you feel rich inside and out.

www.tarawinters.com.au
@tarawinters.co

Chapter 3

The mid-life sensual awakening

Sonia Bavistock

This chapter is dedicated to the women who are ready to see how good it can really get.

A funny thing happened to me on my way to age thirty: I lost my libido.

I say "lost" as if it were a thing—like losing my keys or the back of an earring or my favourite pen.

And it was in this labelling of "losing my libido" that I inadvertently did a powerful thing. I disempowered myself by disconnecting parts of myself and making them separate from me. I didn't see it or realise it at the time, but it would be revealed to me in numerous ways over a decade later when, aged thirty-eight, I would experience my *sensual awakening*.

We'll get to that in a moment. First, there's a backstory to tell.

At the age of twenty-five, I experienced a change in my cycle and my hormones, which led me down a four-year path of doctors, specialists, tests and experiments that ultimately yielded no clear answers and no real solutions. Instead, it exacerbated the disconnected feeling I had created within myself from the waist down. I used to describe this as though someone had pulled apart two power cords at my solar plexus. My chakras from the heart upwards stayed online. The ones below went offline. And what I recognise now, all these years later, is that in those tender early uncertain and unsettling years of that change happening to me, I not only forgot that I was still a sexual being (libido or no libido), but I also forgot how to access joy, fun, and ultimately pleasure. Back then, I was just fixated on the fact that I struggled to feel turned on in my body, despite having a beautiful life, an amazing husband and an abundance of love. I had nothing to complain about … so what the heck was wrong with me?

It's so interesting when something unexpected like this happens to us, especially when it comes to women and our hormones. It's as if a different coloured filter is put over the lens of our perspective and suddenly, in an instant, we feel different and our world looks different to us. We must figure out who we are now in this new skin and how we move through our lives with this new viewpoint. Priorities change. This newness is all we know now and all we notice. So, we close the energetic tabs on the elements of who we used to be BC (before the change). Take me, for example. I couldn't possibly be Sexy Sonia, Sensual Sonia, Confident Sonia or Playful Sonia. I didn't know how to access any of those versions of myself anymore. They were programmed into my DNA, I knew that, but I just couldn't find the files to save myself.

Between the ages of twenty-five and thirty-eight, I tried everything inside and outside the medical arena. I did what the doctors and specialists told me to do, but that didn't work. So, I looked elsewhere and worked with naturopaths, osteopaths, nutritionists, physiotherapists, massage therapists, talk therapists, somatic therapists, coaches, mentors and more.

I tried all the things—detoxes, diets, meditation, movement, self-pleasure practices—you name it, I did it. But after thirteen years of non-stop trying, I was just so done with it all and I found myself in a new place: *acceptance*. Maybe this was just who I was now and how my body was going to be. Maybe this was my life now, my new reality and my job was to find my place in it.

Shortly after I begrudgingly made this sad and silent pact masquerading as inner peace, I found myself on the other end of an unflinchingly honest conversation with one of my best friends. I stripped my soul bare and revealed to her I was just so sick of feeling the way I'd been feeling all these years. Nothing had really changed. Nothing had actually worked. Nothing had truly shifted. I was tired of feeling this way. Exhausted, even.

I told her that I was no longer available for the garbage story I had written and subscribed to. I was beyond done with thinking this was all there was for me and this was as good as it gets. I began to wonder and question what more and better could look like for me.

There must have been some kind of cosmic magic and divine timing at play because in that moment of speaking my deep dark truth out loud, I suddenly sensed something different that hadn't been there before. It was like a door had cracked open just wide enough for me to notice it was there … and to see the tiniest shard of light tenderly shining through the gap.

It was enough of a catalyst to put a plan in place. This time, I wasn't going to outsource by hiring any experts. I was done with looking outside of myself for the answers and putting other people on a power pedestal. This time, I would trust my own inner guidance. And so began a personal journey I nicknamed "Project Radiance". For six weeks, I focused on key areas of my life and committed myself to tiny daily actions that would align me with the energy of the woman I wanted to be and knew I could be. A reconnection with and a reclamation and liberation of my radiance, my confidence and my sensuality.

This was an experiment, sure, as I let my mind form the plan, let my body take the action and trusted my intuition to guide me along the way but at its truest core, it was a playful exploration of allowing myself to have fun with expressing my identity as a woman, as Sonia, age thirty-eight.

The results were immediate, mind-blowing and obvious not only to myself but to everyone around me.

First, I began to dress differently. I pause here because the power of how we choose to express ourselves through clothing is not to be underestimated. We can either blend in, be unnoticed and disguise who we really are, or we can be a true and technicolour external representation of our inner cells that sparkle and pulsate underneath the layers of fabric we decide to wear. Obviously, I chose the latter. And so, I started to put together different combinations of my clothes to create fresh new outfits—clothes that I could no longer hide myself behind. It became an art form and a joyful ritual for me; one I used to do all the time in my former life as a fashion and lifestyle blogger. From here, I made daily decisions about how I desired to adorn my body with makeup and jewellery. If it felt good, I went with it.

This seemingly simple act had a ripple effect that played out in every other aspect of my life, internally and externally. I began to hold myself differently. I sat upright. I stood taller. I held eye contact with people. I smiled more widely and I laughed at full volume. I ate what I felt like and stopped when I was satisfied. I switched up the music I listened to, introducing more vibey tunes that automatically made me want to move my hips. I started to fall in love with exercise and going to the gym, marvelling at the strength of my wondrously resilient body and at how amazing I felt after a training session. I booked monthly bodywork sessions to tend to my poor, fried nervous system and let my body gently feel, heal and release. I stopped doing things in my business that everyone else had told me to do and recommitted myself to my original love of writing and storytelling.

In this process of doing away with old ways of being and doing things my way, I began to share this new personal project of mine with my social media community, and a beautiful and unexpected thing happened. I received messages from women also in their late thirties (and older)—many of whom had never commented on a post, let alone reached out to me before—saying that they too were in the early stages of their own sensual awakening and had yet to put a name or words to it. Let alone speak to anyone else about it.

At this point, I realised I had started a conversation I didn't expect to be having with anyone other than myself, my husband, and my closest girlfriends. Yet here I was, becoming an online poster girl for women just like me, accidentally on purpose. I say "accidentally on purpose" because social media is an intimately familiar landscape to me. I've been on Instagram since its early days and have been fortunate to build not one but two amazing communities on the platform: the first with my fashion and lifestyle blog, and the second with my coaching and mentoring business. So, it never occurred to me to *not* share my journey. I'm simply a storyteller no matter where I am or what I'm doing.

But the overwhelmingly raw and honest and heartbreakingly beautiful messages from these women blew me away. They thanked me for talking about what I was moving through, they applauded my openness, they celebrated my emergence, they loved my new vibe … and they asked for more. OK. Wow. This was really happening. I was really doing this. Not just for me, but for these gorgeous women in my global digital community. I was illuminating a middle chapter of our lives as women that was previously skipped over, not spoken about and kept hidden in the shadows. I was the connecting thread between us and my mission was to paint this invisible thread gold.

So, if I was to be—for want of a better term—the "mid-life sensual poster girl" for us, surely there was a super strong representation of this online: late-thirties women exploring their sensuality and style, sharing their journey, and leading the charge … right? Well, it's so interesting to note what happened next. You know when you buy a new car and suddenly you see it everywhere? The same thing happened online. Something that hadn't been on my radar was suddenly splashed across my feed. The examples of sensuality I wanted to see of women just like me (especially ones around my age, size and body shape) were hard to come by. If I wanted the same old sensual cliché to model my awakening on, that was easy to find. And let's be real, it should come as an Instagram Sensuality Starter Kit—black lace lingerie, long-stemmed red rose, wide-brimmed hat and high-heeled boots included. Pout sold separately.

I was looking for the antidote to this. Forget internet sensuality, I was looking for everyday sensuality.

I realised it had to start with a clean slate so I could write my own personal definition and have a representation of my own design. It had to start with me. So, what did it mean to me to be a sensual woman? Immediately, I tuned into a vision of a woman who knows herself deeply and is comfortable in her skin. She has a quiet confidence and trusts herself. She isn't led by trends; she is guided by what she loves and what feels most like her. She rests into her essence and exudes earthy femininity. She is playful, fun, joyful. Unafraid and unapologetic. And boy oh boy, is that sexy.

This is when I began to understand that—as women—we source our radiance, our lifeforce, our vitality, our zest for life and yes, our sexuality and our sensuality from deep within. It is, quite literally, encoded in our DNA. It snaps, pops and crackles in our cells. It flows through our veins and vibrates in our frequency. This is where our sovereignty lives. This is where we access our personal power. It is who we always have been and always will be. It is who we truly are.

The six weeks of my "Project Radiance" were merely the beginning of this unlearning and remembering. A rediscovery of Sonia, through the lens of today. The results I created are not magical or revolutionary. There was not one key thing that unlocked the change I so deeply desired for myself for thirteen years. It was everything and all of it that led me here. But most of all—I was completely, totally and utterly ready to change. I was locked into my decision and devoted to following its thread.

There's a quote attributed to the universe that says, *'I had to make you uncomfortable, otherwise you never would have moved.'* No truer words. Also, well played universe, because it was that switch that flipped, the disconnection that took place, and the dark early days that followed that lit a tiny spark within me, accompanied by a curiosity that perhaps there really could be more and better for me on the path ahead. The path that led me back to myself.

One of my earliest memories is as a three-year-old girl. On holiday at a theme park with my family, I eagerly volunteered to join the band on stage for their final number and found myself, a mini wannabe Stevie Nicks, tambourine in hand, bopping along to a song I have never been able to recall. What I do remember, though, is how I felt. Elated. Joyful. It was amazing. So much fun! I had absolutely no idea what I was doing—I love music but cannot sing or play an instrument—but I didn't care. I simply said yes to the opportunity without a worry in the world or thought of how anyone might judge me. I just jumped in and went with it. I recall afterwards there was applause and tourists gathered around the stage, asking my parents if they could take photos of me. Mind you, this was the late eighties, and I can assure you it was way less weird than it sounds. But isn't it just so wild to remember how we used to be just like this when we were young? Open. Curious. Playful. Free.

Fast forward to adulthood—womanhood—and so many of our childlike qualities seem to get squashed down inside us and shoved into a deep dark corner of our being, rarely brought out into the light. We don't allow ourselves to be silly for fear of others not taking us seriously. We say no instead of yes to opportunities because we don't consider ourselves worthy or qualified enough. We don't do things just for the fun of it because there's no time and those things don't make us money. We stay small and quiet because we worry about what people will think of us if we take up more space and say what we really mean. We don't just jump in and go for it, because where will that lead us ...?

What we need to realise is that so much of getting older is coming back to the things we loved and who we were when we were young. It's the gift of giving less f**ks and being more of who we truly are. It's in the reclamation of all the parts and pieces of us that we've discarded along the way and recognising that every aspect of us is what makes us who we are. Mid-life is a season of womanhood where we are old enough to have the wisdom of experience but still young enough to have so much more exploration and discovery ahead of us. This is no longer the time of the "invisible woman"—this is the era of the "awakening woman". So, who are you? Who do you want to be? There's still time. It's not too late.

What passions and pastimes were you drawn to as a child?

Which of those call you still?

What lights you up and brings you joy? How is that represented in your life today?

If time and money were no object, what would you do just for fun?

What is your relationship with pleasure? How do you receive life?

The answers to these questions will tell you more about yourself than any expert can. They will give you a roadmap to your core essence. To your happiness. Your vitality. Your creativity. Your sensuality. Here, you'll forget all the advice you gathered along the way; all the misdirections and detours that took you off your own path and you'll lead yourself back onto your own. You'll remember who the f**k you are, and you'll truly begin to love and appreciate her. You'll trust in yourself, believe in yourself and back yourself like never before. And if you need living proof, revisit this chapter and remember me.

There is no silver bullet to being or having more of anything we desire. There's no one single thing that changes it all for us. Everything we've tried and tested in the past has contributed to who we are and where we find ourselves today. It all matters. It all counts. The real magic is in the deciding. Of truly being done with the past and open to the future. Of being completely, totally and utterly ready to change. Of being open and curious and receptive to more and different. And being willing to do the tiny daily actions of the woman we want to be and know we can be. Day in. Day out. Every day. For the rest of our lives, from here on out.

To come back to where this story began: I never "lost" my libido.

What really changed the game for me was realising that I am a sexual and sensual woman by nature. It is who I am, it is my essence, and it can never be taken away from me. Yes, there will be times when my sensuality will be harder to access because of circumstance, stress or whatever life throws at me—but it's still there and will always be there because I am me.

A sensual woman.

And my best is yet to come.

About the author

Sonia Bavistock

Sonia Bavistock is a former communications manager and lifestyle blogger turned mentor, speaker and writer, who has been heart-led throughout her entire life by her undeniable love of storytelling. She works with women across the globe who are leading conscious families, workplaces, communities, and businesses to enrich the world in exquisite and meaningful ways in the realms of self-awareness, confidence, expression and creativity. She is on a mission to hand out as many permission slips as possible to women everywhere to activate who they truly are and live an audaciously full and beautiful life built from their own desires. Sonia is wife to Chris, mum to fur kids Amalfi and Sebby, and lives in the Northern Rivers of NSW.

www.soniabavistock.com
@sonia.bavistock

Chapter 4

The first year

Hannah Thomas

To Isabelle, on her first birthday.

Soon it will be our daughter's first birthday. Like many parents, this is the time we start thinking about what we might like to do to mark this special day. A time to reflect on all we have experienced and learned during our first year together. Except we have lived just *one day* of that year holding our daughter in our arms. I would choose to live that day over and over again just to hold her again.

I'm an ordinary person fortunate to have found a special person with whom to share my life. One dream for our shared lives has always been to create a family together and raise children. To be someone's parent and to parent alongside each other. The collective wisdom we'd received was that it would be one of the hardest and most fulfilling roles of our lives. We began this journey to make a family of our own some years ago. We found a place to call home and later welcomed an exuberant golden retriever we named Abbey. We've delighted in and loved her immensely every day since.

We tried for a baby. One year later, we fell pregnant for the first time. Not with just one, but two precious babies—identical twins. We navigated those early weeks of pregnancy watching their tiny little hearts beat beautifully on the ultrasound screen, feeling equal parts surprise, anticipation and trepidation. It made me think a lot about my grandmother who was a triplet, born in 1924. I wondered about her own mother's experience of a multiple pregnancy in a rural country town nearly one hundred years ago. With modern advances, our experience paled in comparison. In those early appointments, we learned our twins shared a placenta, but each had their own amniotic sacs (known as MCDA twins). We eagerly asked questions about what we could see and enquired about what we might expect in the weeks to come. We were initially a little worried that one twin was slightly smaller, and their heart was beating slower than the other. The sonographer reassured us that everything looked well. They shared that their own identical twins were now eleven years old, and that one had always been a little smaller than the other. This was the first time we started to think about what might be about to unfold before us. It was surreal. I felt pure amazement at what the human body, my body, could do. I'll forever be grateful for my husband's keen interest and engagement during those weeks. He researched everything there was to know about MCDA twins and all that could be done to ensure the safety of mum and babies throughout the pregnancy. Almost daily, he sweetly expressed his concern about how he would ever tell them apart. We smiled together and agreed that we'd work it out.

Days later, the pregnancy was over. With no warning or indication anything was wrong, our twins' hearts had stopped beating just shy of ten weeks' gestation. Our lives collided with the heartbreak of miscarriage. While we knew there was an increased risk of this for MCDA twins, investigations could find no obvious reason. We now know them as our identical twin boys. Having only just overcome the challenges of falling pregnant, losing them was what we feared most. Yet this was now something we had no choice but to accept. Their little lives had ended. We were offered the standard advice to put it down to "bad luck", that "our prospects were good", and to "keep trying". We did just that.

Our second pregnancy was different. Just one baby. I had the familiar discomfort of nausea and vomiting throughout the pregnancy. I told myself that in the end it would all be worth it, which it absolutely was. This time, some things were also the same. We had another devastating and unexplained ending outside our control. Six months into the pregnancy, we again heard the words no parent wants to hear.

'I can't find a heartbeat.'

Forty hours after finding out our baby had died, our daughter was born. We named her Isabelle Dolly. She was small, perfect and still—ten tiny fingers, and ten tiny toes. She had wideset eyes and a low brow like her dad, thin lips and long limbs like me. Like all parents there is a distinct affinity to life before and after Isabelle was born. There will always be an Isabelle-shaped hole in our lives to navigate. I'm grateful that I could give Isabelle a peaceful and gentle entrance to the world. Her birth went as well as you could ever hope one like this could go, thanks in a large way to our excellent care team making it a physically and emotionally safe experience. No amount of time with Isabelle was ever going to be enough, though we are deeply thankful for the time we did get. We spent time with her, making memories we will hold for our lifetimes. We also decided to introduce Isabelle to her four grandparents, which was a highlight. Between the profound sadness and sheer pride of meeting and holding her, somehow, we found the courage to say goodbye to Isabelle's tiny body. The greatest act of love we could ever give her. The most heart-wrenching moment was deciding the moment had arrived, and to inform the midwife we were ready for Isabelle to be taken to the morgue. We walked out of the hospital into the cold evening air shattered, completely lost and unsure about how we would find a way forward. No baby in my tummy, no baby in our arms. The soft brown eyes and wagging tail that met us on our return home was the warmest of comforts. We were met with the same joy of a reunion like any other day. We let Abbey smell every little bit of Isabelle that she could find on us.

Our experience of parenthood has been profoundly different to what we ever could have expected. Instead of a year of seeing our baby grow older and reach new milestones, it has been a first year of beginning to integrate the loss of our precious daughter. Working out what life looks like when you carry children in your heart and not your arms. The experience of bereaved parenthood is a narrative that can be almost invisible. Partly because of how deeply personal it is, but largely because of the stark taboo society places on open conversations about the death of a baby. This is compounded by the general difficulty we have with expressions of grief of any kind in our society. Those around are uncertain of how best to offer support, or there is a misguided and unspoken perception that grief has a predefined expiry date, or that somehow time alone heals all wounds. It makes complete sense why it doesn't feel overly safe for the bereaved to share. The added tragedy of the primary loss of loved ones is that it comes with this secondary loss that makes the experience of living with grief that much more isolating when lumped on top of the already heavy and exhausting load. While this is true for any loss, there is, of course, nuance in each type of loss. Each of our lives started in the same way, inside a womb. In this way, it is curious how assumptions can unfortunately misrepresent the experience of those touched by baby loss. This is important because it directly translates to how we support and offer comfort to ourselves and those around us when these types of losses occur, which they frequently do.

The unique aspect of baby loss is that there are so few memories to sustain you and no tangible sense of that little person's identity, and what kind of mark they might have made on the world had they been able to stay. It is all just out of reach. Everything that ought to have been, simply isn't. In so many ways, it is about every one of us fully embracing the idea that we can't always make things right. We have to learn to be with what is. Witness and not rescue. There is no making it better by saying the exact right thing. We also do more damage by staying silent. The way to offer kindness and respect for what cannot be resumed is to awkwardly sit with what is and not be tempted to try to make it smaller, clean it up, or make it go away. That is what helps.

Loss makes us justifiably and very helpfully emotionally uncomfortable. The sadness tells us how important our lost loved one is to us. These feelings are not something to be feared or apprehensive about, nor should they be something to be minimised or suppressed, and least of all conquered. The experience of grief is something truly remarkable and beautiful if we can give it the time and space to teach and connect us. It adds richness, texture and colour to life in deeply meaningful ways. It is an opportunity to have our perspectives challenged, be more mindful, live more intentionally, use our time wisely, have more tender conversations, and ultimately to learn to sit with the experience of painful and profound grief. That is much of what this past year has been like.

After losing our twins, an undeniable protective mechanism kicked in to try to offer a softer landing should we encounter another loss. Past pain is never forgotten. It was hard to fully embrace that this second pregnancy was happening, and that we had now reached further than we had with the twins. What we saw others do was now, in fact, happening for us. It was distinctly uncomfortable but overwhelmingly wonderful. During Isabelle's pregnancy, I remember expressing to my husband on numerous occasions how much I deeply hoped everything was OK as I didn't really have any tangible ways of knowing something might be wrong. As the pregnancy progressed, I gently and eventually let myself fully realise that there was in fact this beautiful life growing inside me. With each week and each scan, we saw our precious baby wriggling around on a screen, which was backed up by the medical reassurance that all continued to be well. We counted down the weeks until we would meet. After around twenty weeks, I'd started to say jubilantly to my husband how this baby was ours, and ours forever, and how much I was looking forward to starting to feel more definitive movement in my tummy. A swell of mixed feelings. We decided not to find out the gender. It was to be a wonderful surprise to look forward to at the birth. Investigations after Isabelle was born indicated that her growth slowed, that eventually her just heart stopped beating. No indication and no identifiable explanation. We can only surmise as to what might have happened, but no definitive cause. This crushed any sense of us ever being able to reach a safe zone in a pregnancy.

Each of our lives is entwined in the experience of time. Pregnancy, by definition, is about life. Pregnancy loss is an experience of death within our own bodies. The experience of having carried the life and death of a child. For their death to have happened before their birth in an out-of-order way brings a deeper awareness of how limited time defines us all. It is yet another experience that highlights how truly miraculous it is to be granted any time at all. Most of us have, and will face, adverse experiences in our lives. No one can get through life without tragedy and pain. As humans, we are meaning makers, and we develop personal meaning from our experiences which tells us that we all have valuable stories to share. We connect through our shared experiences, our common humanity, and through normalising conversations about the experience and impact of challenging times. Being heard offers an opportunity for compassion and understanding, and for exquisite meaning making and connection. Life is meant to be felt. Our feelings are meant to be expressed. Joy can coexist alongside sadness. The beauty of being human is that we get to feel both. We are multidimensional and can hold two feelings sometimes opposing, at the very same time. In doing this, we can then let our grief be a life companion and learn that it is really just another form of love. We are not meant to care for ourselves alone through loss and adversity. It is not meant to be the lone task of an individual. We must learn to be with that pain when it occurs in ourselves and when we see it in others. To ultimately be at peace with the discomfort of being human. We can do better than to let grief be a silent load. A simple 'How are you?' is a far from simple question to answer. Yet so commonly we answer it politely and plainly, sometimes because it is not the appropriate time or place. But I urge us all to slow down enough to offer safety and opportunity to hear the honest answer. Because even when we seem OK, it is of great comfort when others check in.

Isabelle is not an event that happened to us, she is our daughter. It warms my heart to have her name written or spoken, to have others ask about her and talk about her openly, ideally unprompted. It most definitely doesn't make me feel sadder, and instead makes the love we have for her emanate even more widely and lets her life touch others' lives. This is the only way we get to share her outside of us, like we would have if she had the chance to grow older. Most of all, it helps me to feel close with her and to honour her memory. The two things I feel most compelled to protect as her mum. Grief offers me that.

Even though one baby never replaces another, it was hard to acknowledge how deeply I longed for another daughter. We continued to work towards expanding our family. New doctors, new clinics, and new treatments. More waiting and hoping. An experience more gruelling than the last. We fell pregnant a third time. This time, I decided I wanted to fully embrace the reality of this pregnancy right from the start. I was determined to make the most of this time by taking many more photos in particular, knowing now how precious they are to us, after having so few of Isabelle's pregnancy. All while desperately hoping for a forty-week pregnancy, a healthy baby and a long lifetime with them thereafter. We had ten weeks with Isabelle's baby sister before we lost her, too. It cannot be explained why she didn't get the chance to stay either. Those were the most anxious weeks of my entire life, but I hold those precious memories of time with Isabelle's sister just as fondly.

Grief is a deep ache, such a profound sadness. The grief continues as time goes on. It continues to evolve. It can be activated in surprising new ways and at unexpected times. Grief is a reality to move forward with, not a feeling to be overcome. This is living with grief. The more time that passes the more you live of what your children don't get to experience. We are grieving our path to parenthood and multiple imagined futures that didn't get to be. We accept that. We don't fight it, but it still hurts. We all have depths that would do well to be expressed, held space for, and heard compassionately. This adds richness, nuance and can generate connections that can strengthen us in ways we could never imagine. Grieving is personal, it's unstructured and non-linear. It is like returning many times to the same spot to contemplate and try to come to terms with what has happened, and what is now happening. Then, trying as you might to figure out your next steps. Loss hurts and grief is heavy to carry, but it helpfully keeps us connected to our children and the love we hold for them.

The meaning drawn from any experience offers new and deepened perspectives. That is what lived experience does. This doesn't mean there is a clear and defined upside. The loss of our much loved and longed for children is absolutely awful, agonisingly sad and excruciatingly cruel. The seemingly endless wait, the intensity of the medical treatments and procedures, the heaviness of the compounding grief, the anxiety of a new pregnancy is the path we choose to walk to try to bring home a living child. These are all elements of time we must sit with. There is immense uncertainty. There are no guarantees. We accept that, but it still hurts. All of this doesn't mean there is no joy to be experienced or hope to hold on to. All we can do is try to face reality with courage, embrace all the feelings that arise, focus on what is in within our control, and decide on the next best step forward in the moment in front of us. What undoubtedly also helps is when others witness that pain with us.

In the hardest of times, when we face some of the greatest life transitions and transformations, it is much less isolating when it happens in the company of others. I continue to feel deep gratitude and liberation in building connections with those who are walking similar journeys. A whole community of bereaved parents, a community whom we never knew existed that welcomes new families every day. Through books, websites, social media, podcasts, support groups, walks, coffee dates, yoga sessions, fundraisers, special events, holidays and anniversaries, we have connected with other parents like us. Parents in the same postcode, as well as those on the other side of the country and across the globe. Something we are fortunate to have in today's world. This network has grounded me immensely. Most touchingly, you hear more stories of other children not in their loving parents' arms. These children I call Isabelle's friends. The friendship and bond with other loss mums, in particular, I treasure dearly. The gift of their presence has allowed me to share just how much I'm hurting. They are at ease with all iterations of tears and anguish (and dark humour). All while carrying their own grief often just as new as mine.

We are all hurting. I am grateful we have been able to hold space for each other's unique experiences and build a connection around our shared motherhoods. These women are the kind that turn up on your doorstep at short notice when your family's story has taken yet another hard turn. They give freely. They show up with flowers, care packages, and the warmest of hugs, making you feel seen when you feel like the world has swallowed you up. It offers an opportunity to express what your experience really is. Where you don't have to cushion your feelings to protect yourself from others' reactions. This opportunity to fully feel and connect is how we find the courage to keep moving forward. We are brave, scared and fearless, grieving and hopeful all at once. Our grief is the love deeply felt, the loved shared and the love that will endure.

About the author

Hannah Thomas

Hannah is a mum living inside grief. Her new life companion. She believes in tender conversations because they help us express our pain. It can offer us a moment to be heard and acknowledged. She has learned first-hand how, in safe and connected moments, pain can be released and begin to move. She ponders that with this perhaps we will all master the narrative of our own stories.

@mama_to_isabelle

Chapter 5

Embracing the power of internal safety

Kate Jones

For all those on the cusp of audacious curiosity

How often in your daily life do you find yourself wondering, '*Is this a challenge, or is it a cosmic nudge beckoning me to stretch my boundaries?*' These are the moments, often cloaked in discomfort, that bear the most precious lessons. But discomfort isn't always a bad thing. What if it's your innate, all-knowing self, pushing you out of your comfort zone and into the wild unknown? It's like my mentor always says, 'Nothing changes until the cost of staying the same becomes too great.' It's in those moments when we find ourselves facing a choice: to hunker down and resist or to lean in and grow. Now that I have created the "Sacred Living Process" and know what it means to "lean in and grow" and how to actually do that, I don't ever want to stay stagnant when there's a whole universe of personal growth waiting to be explored.

These moments, the ones that make us squirm and question everything, they're not just hurdles to overcome. They're secret doorways, inviting us to tap into our hidden superpowers. Giving us access to inner strengths we didn't even know we had until life threw us a curveball. They're our chances to say, '*You know what, discomfort? Bring it on. I'm ready to step up.*'

Embracing these moments isn't just about us as individuals.

We're all in on this cosmic dance together. We're part of a much larger story, a story of unity that ties humanity together. It's about replacing judgment with understanding, isolation with community and fear with compassion. Each interaction, each encounter, becomes a piece of this intricate puzzle we're all working on.

Embracing the Unknown: My Journey to Peru
Let's rewind a bit. My journey into the world of embracing discomfort led me to a place I never thought I'd go: the sacred landscapes of Peru. I wasn't one to just hop on a plane to unknown lands with strangers from all corners of the globe. But something about this offer set my Spidey senses on fire. I just knew I had to go. They say life begins at the edge of your comfort zone. Well, this idea of going to Peru was a whole new realm for me as a mum of two young kids.

There I was, in South America, surrounded by women from different walks of life, all united by this common thread of seeking something more. The path ahead was hazy, filled with uncertainty and unpredictability. But I made a pact with myself: I would stay present, let my intuition guide me and allow the journey to unfold as it may with no expectations.

This journey didn't just start the day I boarded that plane. It had been simmering beneath the surface for a while, guided by what I now lovingly call my "Sacred Self". Like I mentioned, this inner knowing or compass kept nudging me towards growth, even when I wasn't fully aware of it. This Sacred, bestest friend possible in the whole universe version of me, had prepared me in its own sneaky way to face the untouched corners of my life that had always seemed a bit too daunting.

Creating Moments of Stillness and Reflection

Life's constant whirlwind often engulfed me in a storm of relentless self-criticism and doubt. Those "mean girl" thoughts seemed like a broken record, replaying my supposed inadequacies and fuelling a sense of unworthiness. And there were those moments when everything spiralled out of control. It was as if molten lava surged through my veins, blurring my vision and shrinking the world around me. An internal scream tightened around my throat, stifling any voice I had. Amid these bursts of frustration, the craving for moments of quiet reflection became an undeniable need—an oasis of stillness to navigate the torrent of emotions that threatened to erupt. Because, honestly, trying to suppress and control them was no longer effective.

A simple question emerged as a lifeline: '*How would I like to feel today?*' It might sound basic, but it became my anchor amidst the chaos. I set aside a mere sixty seconds each morning to connect with my thoughts. Those stolen moments transformed into potent tools, helping me navigate life's labyrinthine lessons with a newfound perspective. It was a way of taming the turmoil that occasionally stormed my day.

Surrounding Myself with Healing Spaces and People

In hindsight, I realised I had underestimated the power of supportive surroundings. My ego fought tooth and nail against joining group sessions, coming up with a myriad of excuses. Only when I exhausted every excuse did I reluctantly give it a try. Looking back, it's clear that stepping into healing spaces and connecting with compassionate souls transformed my journey in ways I hadn't anticipated. The company of kindred spirits who embraced growth as a resounding "yes" to life shifted my path. Slowly, a cocoon of empathy and acceptance formed, a space where I could bare my vulnerabilities. Strangely, even before I consciously knew, something inside me understood that this was what I needed.

Practicing Affirmations and Meditations

Back then, I wasn't constructing pillars of self-love or self-worth. I was just building my way forward. I started a daily ritual, setting hourly alarms on my phone as gentle nudges. Each chime reminded me to recite affirmations: 'I love you. I am precious. I am safe. I forgive you. I am a soul in a body. Only love is real.' I repeated these words seven times, slowly etching them into my soul. These moments of dedication became a key to unlock my internal sanctuary, nurturing its growth.

Challenging Self-Limiting Beliefs

This journey wasn't just about new habits; it was about confronting old, self-imposed limitations. I faced beliefs that had shackled me for years, remnants of childhood experiences and the fear of the unknown. As I tackled them head-on, I also offered forgiveness to my past self, acknowledging that I didn't know any better. Those fears had kept me on a restricted path, but confronting them allowed me to rewrite the script with positive forward momentum.

Taking Small Steps Towards Growth

I didn't need to take monumental leaps into the unknown. Instead, I embraced the power of small shifts. Each one felt like adding a piece to a mosaic of personal evolution. Each step, no matter how seemingly minor, uncovered more of my authentic self. With each challenge I conquered, my confidence grew, giving me the courage to face even greater obstacles. This journey of steady progress, every step acknowledged and celebrated, culminated in a transformation that, looking back, defied quantification.

Embracing Discomfort as a Gateway to Growth

As I embraced the art of self-nurturing, my relationship with discomfort transformed. It was no longer an enemy but a portal to growth. I realised that real evolution often resides beyond the comforts we cling to, in the enigmatic realm of the unknown. This understanding brought with it the promise of healing and self-discovery.

And then, all along, as I navigated my everyday existence, I was unknowingly preparing for the life-altering voyage that awaited in Peru. Shedding the weight of self-doubt and fear, I nurtured an internal sanctuary of strength. It was this sanctuary that gave me the courage to embark on the uncharted journey, one that would redefine my understanding of the dance between internal safety and unity.

Boarding the plane bound for Peru, a sense of anticipation and excitement welled up within me. Instinctively, I understood this journey would inscribe itself as a defining chapter, forever altering my understanding of the delicate interplay between heeding the wisdom of my Sacred Self and the profound influence of human connection.

Experiencing the Transformative Adventure in Peru

Peru welcomed me with open arms, thrusting me into the company of strangers who would soon become pivotal to a transformative moment. While the uncertainty of the journey initially stirred discomfort, it was soon replaced with a sense of belonging as connections blossomed and trust deepened over the three weeks.

The pinnacle of our trip led us into the heart of the Amazon. Deep within its impenetrable wilderness, the experience took root. Here, where the chorus of wildlife created an enchanting cacophony and tarantulas ventured within arm's reach, the Shaman resided in a humble tin-roofed dwelling. This place was untouched by electricity or plumbing, isolated from civilization's trappings, and accessible solely by boat. A ninety-minute speedboat journey unveiled our accommodation, nestled in the embrace of the jungle, almost concealed beside the flowing river.

Encountering the lead shaman here and immersing myself in his ancient traditions infused me with hope—a glimmer that this experience might provide the missing puzzle piece in my quest for self-realisation and purpose. Little did I grasp that the unfolding journey was merely beginning its course.

The ceremonial hut was nestled within the dense Amazon rainforest, its presence concealed by the canopy's immensity shielding the world below. Approaching the hut involved crossing a delicate walkway suspended above the ground, a necessary elevation designed to combat the river's periodic swells. At dusk, the jungle came alive with an overwhelming orchestra, the incessant chirping of insects, the calls of exotic birds, and the distant roars of creatures unidentifiable to foreign ears. This auditory tapestry was matched by a visual curtain of darkness that fell, rendering the world outside an impenetrable black. Inside, the hut held its own set of surprises, such as the gentle frog—a symbol of good fortune, and a swift tarantula, its movements so quick it became a mere blur, as the caretakers gently nudged it, careful not to harm its intricate feet. Yet, amid these vibrant details, the focal point remained the Shaman and the impending ritual. An initiation began by ingesting a liquid so repulsive, its taste could only be described as a challenge in itself. A thin but potent brown liquid that could be smelt well before it reached my lips was served from a well-used, stained, plastic milk bottle. Consciously deciding before it was my turn not to pause for an extra whiff, I glugged down a flat white's worth of the foulest, most repulsive tonic ever created.

The lead shaman stood before us, a figure of unassuming stature. His head barely reached my shoulder as he communicated through fluid gestures and imparted wisdom in his native tongue. Dressed in simple, well-worn attire, he defied the stereotype of a "holy" man. His skin, demeanour and body language portrayed a life immersed in the everyday rhythms of the village, much like any other member. However, his role as a shaman was unmistakable in the mastery he exuded and the reverence he commanded. At his side stood a female shaman, equally adept, a living testament to his guidance, lineage and the shared traditions they embodied.

As night brought its impenetrable blackness, our first evening's Ayahuasca ceremony unfolded. Suddenly, a profound sense of aloneness and vulnerability washed over me, and fear began to tighten its familiar grip, strangling any attempt to release the reality and identity I had spent a lifetime perfecting. Emotions surged within me like turbulent waves, caught between frustration and anger. While others appeared to effortlessly journey into realms of profound insight, I felt ensnared by my feelings of inadequacy and disappointment. The elusive ideals of relaxation and surrender danced just beyond my reach, intensifying my sense of disconnection. It seemed as though a profound mystery was unfolding for others, while I remained stranded on the shores of comprehension.

Now, as a life coach and facilitator of women's groups, I've come to recognise how the comparison of others' experiences to our own can hinder our growth. Our perception of how others' journeys unfold and the intensity or ease we perceive through the lenses of our own self-doubt often creates an internal projection of not being enough or not being good enough, as though we are failing in our own personal development. This sense of lack only deepens the disconnect.

This is where the power of the group and the willingness to show up come into play. It's in the continued act of showing up that individuals can begin to untangle the tethers that anchor them to their self-limiting beliefs. Together, within the safe and supportive space of the group, we learn that our journeys are unique, that growth is nonlinear, and that the richness of our experiences lies not in how they compare to others but in our willingness to explore them fully. It's a journey of self-discovery, where we shed the weight of comparison and embrace the lightness of authenticity.

My familiar, distressing feelings of entrapment, with no apparent escape, began to simmer within me. All I yearned for was to flee. To escape this room, evade the watchful eyes, and distance myself from the looming darkness that cradled my painful secrets, shame and sorrow. The urge to run, to avoid its impending embrace, was overwhelming. It sat there, a formidable challenge, daring me to let it surface and engulf me entirely. It all became too much and silent tears streamed down my cheeks, mirroring the weight of my inner turmoil.

The first birdsong of the day offered little solace as the expanding cocktail of disappointment and shame for not living up to my own expectations cloaked me. I grappled with the vast divide between what I had yearned for—transformation and connection—and the haunting shadows of my limitations that I had encountered.

The night stretched endlessly. The potent atmosphere in the ceremonial hut had an otherworldly quality, as if time had been suspended. As its power ebbed and the ceremony concluded, the other women returned exhausted to their individual spaces to await dawn's first light which was refusing to come . A resolute vow escaped my lips: never again would I subject myself to such inner violence.

By around 5.00 am, exhaustion had woven itself into the very fabric of my being, and emotions raged within me. Seeking solace, I retreated to the familiar embrace of my room. There, in the sanctuary of my hammock, the whispers of the jungle melded with the echoes of my own thoughts, weaving a melody of contemplation and uncertainty.

As the day wore on, I distanced myself from the group, yearning for solitude amidst the vast wilderness. Drawn to a tranquil pool, secluded from the world's gaze, its mirror-like surface was only occasionally broken by the orange and blue dragonflies skimming above. Although fatigue weighed heavily on me from the previous night's tumult, an inexplicable urge took hold. Time and again, I dove deep into the crystalline waters, as if trying to reach an inner clarity that lay hidden within the depths of my own soul.

Earlier, my heart had been shrouded in regret, questioning my choice to embark on this foreign expedition in search of answers. The Shamans' cryptic counsel still echoed in my thoughts, their enigmatic demeanour only heightening my sense of frustration. Yet, as the water embraced me, fragments of their words began to transform my perspective. I focused on my intentions—the very reasons that brought me to this distant land, the emotions I aimed to stir, and the chains of my burdens I hoped to break free from. With every dive and stroke,

I envisioned casting these thoughts into the vast expanse of the Amazon, entrusting the universe to receive and respond.

As the water cradled me, I felt an overwhelming bond to the elements—the nurturing water, the verdant jungle, and the vast expanse of sky above. Each motion seemed to liberate a fragment of my pent-up angst, allowing the river currents to whisk them away. Resurfacing, each gasp for air was symbolic of my yearning for understanding and peace. A shift, subtle but transformative, began to settle within me. It felt as though the water's embrace had unveiled a lens, allowing me to perceive the world, and myself, with newfound clarity.

In the delicate balance of twilight, I made a conscious, rebellious decision. Rather than flee from my emotions of shame and desolation, I would confront and immerse myself in them. It was within this embrace of vulnerability that I began to comprehend the true nature of resilience and inner sanctuary. It wasn't about evading the storm but journeying through it, acknowledging its might, yet emerging on the other side, fortified and enlightened. As I closed the door to my room and walked down the corrugated vine bridges to reconnect with the group, a promising hope kindled within me, fortifying my resolve to venture into the ceremony once more that evening, to surrender to the experience, to seek the answers within.

As the cosmos aligned, a sense of anticipation mingled with the evening breeze. The atmosphere was charged with an electric energy as if brimming with the forces of celestial beings who knew that this ceremony held the promise of profound transformation. With my heart beating like a drum, I entered the ceremonial space, a sacred cocoon where dimensions converged and souls embarked on inner journeys.

Distinguishing between discomfort and danger forged the foundation for the second night's ceremony—a foundation grounded in an understanding that personal evolution flourishes beyond the constraints of comfort. As I settled onto the mat, the Shaman's voice resonated, his incantations weaving through the air like tendrils of smoke. The room was illuminated by the soft glow of candlelight, casting dancing shadows on the faces of those gathered.

Throughout that transformative night, I surrendered to the cosmic energies that enveloped me. It was as if time itself unravelled, leaving me suspended in a space where past, present, and future converged. Layer by layer, I shed the emotional weight that had obscured the radiance of my true self. With each release, I felt lighter, as if I was shedding the burdens of lifetimes.

But this night held even more profound moments. I left nothing behind that night. I released and purged everything. The medicines meandering vines unrelentingly penetrated a myriad of my soul's evolutions. Tangling itself around my limitations, fears, and blockages, both past and future, it drew these out of me gently at first. Yet, as the ceremony began its conclusion, it became obvious I wasn't done yet.

The Shaman's focus shifted solely to me, urging me to go deeper, as I visibly struggled to release this final blockage. All the air seemed to escape my lungs as I felt myself being strangled by my own inner demons that refused to leave. All eyes were on me now, as the incantations increased in intensity, filling my head with their pulsating beat, reaching the depths of my being and filling it with the plant medicine's cleansing.

In that moment, my body convulsed as finally, in my mind's eye, I vividly saw a mulberry, globulous energetic form being pulled from me in a flurry and tangle of wings, smoke, and undefinable entities. The ceremony reached its zenith as I collapsed onto the mat, falling into the concerned arms of the woman shaman and the neighbouring woman, both now fully roused from their own experiences.

As I lay still on the mat, stunned by what I had witnessed, I knew something was very different. I felt lighter, not just metaphorically, but as if a heavy weight had been physically lifted from my being. The shackles that had bound me for so long had been broken and I was free.

Simultaneously, I bore witness to the courageous journeys of the diverse women around me, each navigating her unique tangle of experiences. Despite our differences, an unspoken unity enveloped us. In the sacred silence of that moment, I felt the echo of their emotions reverberating within me, weaving an unbreakable thread through our collective tapestry.

This collective experience unveiled shared emotional landscapes and common human struggles. It was as if the barriers that typically separated us had dissolved, leaving us raw and exposed, yet profoundly connected. In our vulnerability, we found strength; in our shared stories, we discovered a universal narrative of growth, healing and transformation.

Working as an energy healer and nurturer of courageous spaces, I often witness this very moment in the women I guide as they teeter on the brink of discovering their own power. It's a delicate dance of fear, oscillating between the comfort of the familiar they're leaving behind and the uncharted territory they're stepping into. This is a battle between the ego's desperate attempts to keep them safe yet stuck, and their all-knowing Sacred Self gently guiding them as they begin to nurture self-trust. As I bear witness to these moments in courageous women who choose to step beyond their discomfort and into a Sacred life they love, I honour their bravery, as I once honoured my own.

As our time in the ceremonial hut drew to a close and the first rays of dawn brushed the sky, I emerged from that sacred space forever changed. The second night had been a portal to the depths of my own soul, a journey through the inner landscapes that had long been hidden from view. In shedding the layers that no longer served me, I had embraced the truth of my own essence—a truth that radiated with a newfound sense of empowerment and self-assurance.

The second night's ceremony had not only been an exploration of the cosmic realms, but also a journey into the heart of my own being. It was a testament to the power of discomfort as a catalyst for growth, and a reminder that true transformation unfolds when we are willing to step beyond the confines of comfort and embrace the uncharted territories of our souls. In this embrace of vulnerability, I realised that the medicine never truly leaves your body, forever entwining with our future pathways in collaboration with our Sacred Self. This profound understanding deepened my connection to the collective experience, reinforcing the idea that we were all on a shared journey, forever connected by the echoes of our emotions and the medicine's enduring presence.

This profound realisation—that beneath the diversity of our lives, we all grapple with similar emotions and experiences—deepened my understanding of unity and empathy. Unburdened by societal expectations and fully aligned with our authentic selves, we gain the capacity to empathise with others' battles, recognizing that their core feelings mirror our own vulnerabilities. Through acknowledging our shared humanity, we foster compassion, understanding and unity.

Conclusion: Embrace Your Journey of Self-Discovery

The journey toward embracing internal safety and unity is a deeply personal one, marked by moments of discomfort and profound healing. As you nurture the flame of your internal sanctuary and venture into the unknown, you traverse the path of growth and thriving. Remember, this journey isn't about reaching an elusive destination; it's about choosing to be present in each moment, embracing each step of the process. Every obstacle is an opportunity for growth, every challenge a chance to expand. As we stretch our individual senses of internal safety and allow our authentic selves to radiate, we create a beacon that resonates with others on similar journeys. Together, we form a collective of empathetic understanding souls, celebrating both our shared humanity and the ripples we create. Through the embrace of internal safety, unity manifests, empowering us to craft a world enveloped in love, understanding and acceptance. So, take that first step, embrace the discomfort and embark on your transformative journey toward internal safety and unity. The world eagerly awaits your light.

About the author

Kate Jones

Kate Jones serves as a Certified Life Coach, Group Facilitator, and the founding visionary behind the transformative "Sacred Living Process". As an energy healer and nurturer of courageous spaces, she emboldens women to rediscover their innate wisdom. Kate's transformative path led her to embrace sacred spaces worldwide, deepening her understanding of internal safety and unity through unlocking self-trust. She resides in Auckland, New Zealand.

www.coaching.katejones.life
@katejones.life

Chapter 6

We're more similar than we're different, especially us women

Tammy Guest

Lying there on the cold table, the gel-covered probe rubbing all over my belly, the smell of Hibiclens up my nose and the radiographer biting her bottom lip with a quizzical look on her face, you could be mistaken for thinking I was about to get the best news of my life. But that was twelve years prior, when I had the privilege of hearing my youngest and final child's heartbeat.

This time in my forties was different; and for all the knowledge of anatomy and physiology from my university degree and time in pathology, my face mirrored the young radiographer's look of bewilderment. The screen seemed to show some very different large masses that I would never find in a Mosby's anatomy textbook.

'That can't be my ovary, can it?' I quizzed.

'Hmmm, when do you go to see your doctor for the results?' she said with a look of concern on her face.

'Not for a fortnight. I'm going away on holidays and figured I'd just go when I got back.'

'Well, they'll be available overnight and I'd suggest you see her as soon as possible. I can't tell you more than that.'

And so the wait began.

As I boarded the plane for Uluru …

If it's the big C, this might be my last flight.

No, it can't be. Maybe it's just inflamed, I've been drinking more than usual lately.

I wonder if this really is the cause of my weight gain, crazy moods and sleep issues.

I told that doctor something was wrong. Why don't they believe us?

No, it will all be fine. I'm just worried about nothing.

Mid holiday, I got to see the scans. They appeared on the online patient portal from the radiography clinic. I must have clicked into and out of that login a hundred times that day.

Oh shit, that really doesn't look right.

Is it my kidney? It's huge.

I have been weeing more lately, especially at night.

Then the wait. Three more days of incessant guessing.

The wait. Is. The. Worst. Although, it gave me plenty of time to reflect on how we got to this place.

After approximately 362 periods and wondered for the hundredth time, '*Really? Now? WTF?*' See, I was ovulating, so '*It shouldn't be showing up like this … and it shouldn't be showing up after a "fun time"*'. In the medical world, this is called a red flag. In the world of endometriosis, PCOS and PMDD, which I have all of, it's a regular issue. In my world, I had reframed it as "an inconvenience". When I was young, I thought this debilitating pain that started in my lower back and radiated down to my knees was normal, and that just as much as no woman wanted to tell you about pads or tampons, they didn't want to tell you about the pain and mental health issues that come around every month.

When I was an athletic teen, I was so excited when my period didn't come because I made it mean I was training hard enough to maintain my slight figure. When I was a young adult, I freaked out that I was pregnant when it didn't come, and I prayed and did deals with God in my mind that if he just let me have my period, I would … In the seven years I was on the pill, "it" came like clockwork, and I didn't have to "worry" anymore. My naturopathic training taught me that pill periods are not actually periods, by the way. The year I tried to fall pregnant, and it just kept coming, I remember crying in many a toilet booth alone. The time I peed on a stick because it didn't arrive, I was so excited in a completely different way. And then the decade and a half since, every single period has brought some of the most intense emotions, mindset challenges and pain, that all the reframing in the world can't stop. The truth is, a red flag is a red flag, and it's screaming to pay attention. '*You're not making it up, you're not weak, there is more investigation needed.*' I didn't get diagnosed with anything until I was thirty-nine, and even then, my first scans were when I was forty.

So, I get home from my holiday to a diagnosis and a plan. Surgery. Leading up to a surgery is hard. The last time I was under general and my body was cut open was as a twelve-year-old for appendicitis. That, I think, manifested because I wanted to get out of PE when I had my period. For the last three days, I've cried in conversations every day with my husband, who's a coach. We've been wonderfully trying to coach the sh&! out of each other. Although, when we both surrendered to an extraordinarily long hug this afternoon, it seemed to feel better. I have skills to deal with this. A wall of qualifications, in body … mind … and spirit … to university level. I can't imagine what this is like for the normal person who doesn't have these tools. And still, it's a big deal. Holding the duality of '*it will be fine, this gynaecological surgeon does this daily*' and '*I am a unique individual with thirty-four centimetres worth of extra stuff in my body that needs to be removed, that by PubMed search could be cancerous due to my age, size of growth and family history.*' The fascinating "Pong" that my mind is masterfully filling my days with … is, well, masterful. It's reframing at its best. I remind myself, '*This too shall pass, and it won't always be this way. Your body will transform, so will your life, so will your relationships, and I know it is always for the better. It's so much bigger, we only realise this in hindsight, and you will be OK.*'

I had my final period party last night. A circle of women, sharing, caring, stories, firsts, lasts, hopes and dreams. We intentionally created sacred smoke wands, choosing plants that represented motherhood, memory and heart. We laughed as everyone sang, 'Happy hysterectomy to you' over an incredible cake that my friend handmade. The cake was uterus shaped and filled with jam, surrounded by the letters "See you later ovulator". I particularly liked the ovary cupcakes. We had special cocktails called "Last Blood". A delightful combination of what looked on the outside to be delicious, but when consumed had a tart sourness followed by a kick. I was blessed with making this moment in my life sacred by honouring and sharing it with like-minded women.

The last thirty-six hours before my surgery had me making the most of my voluptuous body. Voluptuous because my period came the night before my surgery, and my body swells as my period comes through. My period has come at seemingly the most inopportune times in my life, but every single time, on reflection, it's a time when I'm stepping into a new version of me. I'm generally surrounded by women and creating something big, and the old version of me needs to be shed. It's an easy fallback to '*ugh, wtf, not again*' but when I am about to meet my all-female surgical and anaesthetic team, I feel like it's a nod to the next version of me.

My theatre nurse was named Freya, the same name as the Norse goddess of healing.

My anaesthetist told me I needed to think about my favourite place to visit, real or imagined, before I went under. My surgeon agreed to take pictures of my tumours. She understood my wish as we had bonded over my past career in histopathology. A night nurse got me peppermint tea for gas, even though she 'didn't really believe in that stuff'.

Plan Z

I used to be a Plan A type of person. Fly by the seat of my pants and hope for the best. Generally, my manifesting came right on point. Plan B was rarely an option, more of a think-on-your-toes-pivot. And there certainly was no Plan C. Until COVID, and then I planned for C, and continue to do so in the event space I play in. All risk assessments, legals and SOPs are in place for it. I coined the term Plan Z for "zombie apocalypse". What do we do when it all goes to shit? Can't move, locked down, choices out of our control. My husband, Murray, talks to his clients about the Stockdale Paradox. Brutal facts. Sureness of success. The other day, on my healing journey post-surgery, I thought I was cruising along on my Plan A (all is well, healing flow) but I had a Plan Z moment. A newly acquired internet friend wisely said, 'This is what you have been working towards, this exact moment, all that training for now.'

I woke up with the most excruciating pain in all my forty-three years and I couldn't do anything about it. (Except enact everything I had learned from years in medical science and start ticking off a list of possible worst-case scenarios, with my freshly minted "enduring power of attorney" in hand). I headed to emergency. Surrendering to a medical team who didn't want to hear my opinion, through tears, exhaustion and gritted teeth, I advocated to get the tests I needed to rule out worst-case scenarios and then I advocated to get my bum home to heal. It was only three days later they admitted it was the life-saving mixture of antibiotic drugs they put me on that caused a rare reaction of hepatomegaly that pushed on a bunch of nearby tissues and organs, causing excruciating pain.

What does this have to do with Plan Z? Have one, is all I'm saying. Don't hide under the guise of positivity and wishful thinking. You won't manifest bad stuff by simply looking at it … but you will have a plan to create ease and flow if it hits. Look lightly at all the brutal facts yet plan for the sureness of success. Onwards and upwards.

Have you ever wondered?

If we are more microbiome than we are human cells—and I'm wiping out my microbiome within an inch of its life three-hourly with two of the strongest antibiotics on the planet—what consciousness is left? And whose consciousness was I perceiving in the first place if we are all made up of the same subatomic matter? Because I haven't taken pain meds for two days now and my perception is doing some very different things. This healing gig is fascinating.

I've also been wondering how my human body knows where to put everything now so much has been taken out. I mean, that last remnant of ovary could go anywhere. Sure, it still has an abdominal wall ligament, but there's a lot of space. And as for the intestines that made way for all those growths, how do they know to fill up that space in an organised manner?

Hormonally, two-thirds of my female hormone producing tissue has been removed and I wonder how the body decides to rebalance my HPG, HPA and HPT pathways? And if we really want to flip our lids and go full energetic ... technically my root, sacral and solar plexus chakras have all been shaken up ... I wonder about the homeostatic mechanism to have them hum again. Honestly, not looking for solutions, rather marvelling at the innate wisdom of it all. Sitting in awe and wonder as I stare out the window.

The doctor came in yesterday because I had a fever and tachycardia overnight. I felt alright, but everyone seemed a little concerned. Thirty-eight point five degrees centigrade and a resting heart rate of 114 is a bit more than my usual. When she came in, it was my first chance to ask her how it went.

'Well, we had you under for over four hours, so you will be quite sore, and what we thought was in there were actually two huge cysts. One took up your whole right side, from your pelvis to your liver. The other was actually attached to your left ovary but had migrated around your bladder and uterus to also be on your right side. One was filled with hair, teeth and skin cells. It burst as we tried to detach it from your ovary, and although we cleaned it up, your body is now doing the rest of the work to clean up its contents,' she said.

No wonder. It's a shame we all have to wait so long in hospital to understand what's happening, but I am grateful I now do.

'Did you take pictures?' I said.

'Oh yes, and video too, because pictures wouldn't do it justice and it was so interesting,' she said.

At this stage in my healing, I feel a change and feel different. Healing takes time. Like building a business, the thing that works one day isn't what you need the next, but it's the foundation that matters.

Other things I'm noticing … How much energy it takes to just wash my face … then I need a nap.

How exhausting a conversation can be … then I need a nap.

How I basically need a nap after every out-of-the-ordinary move.

I've always told my clients to take naps when they need them, because then we get out of our own way and healing occurs.

So, I'm off to have a nap.

Six months later, I find myself here again, in the pre-op room, with my all-girl team. This time, the rogue ovary, prone to growing tumours is finally coming out. I'm relieved, albeit somewhat worried. Medically induced menopause will begin immediately, and the effects could be challenging. But I'm relieved not to have to guess anymore about the source of my symptoms.

As I lie on the gurney, counting ceiling tiles and pondering the question my anaesthetist asked me last time, I realise the significance of the bargain I made with myself six months ago.

After evaluating my life and asking, *'If I don't wake up from this, and Plan Z actually happens, would I truly be okay with the life I've lived?'* My initial answer before my first surgery was, *'I've achieved everything I set out to do. I changed lives, my family knows they're loved, and I visited 54 countries. If it all turns sour, I'm good and complete.'* But now, in this cold room, I have a massive realisation. *'Hell no, I have so much more to do! I have hopes, dreams, global goals, a capable brain and body, and the blessing of being alive to pursue them.'*

My recovery time was over. As the anaesthetist asked the same question, *'If you could visualise anywhere, real or imagined, what would come to mind?'* The next decades of my life, achievements, milestones and locations flashed before me, like the most exciting personalised movie, and I knew I would wake up a whole new person, ready to take on the rest of my life.

About the author

Tammy Guest

Tammy Guest is a mentor, a speaker and a freedom seeker who takes people on adventures and reminds them how to live. She is also a mother, stepmother, wife, student helicopter pilot, author and artist who believes your business should light you up, not burn you out. It's her mission to remind you of how unique and precious you are, and how important it is to shake things up, tap into who you are and what lights you up, and build a business that aligns with every part of you. Her intention is to empower you to elevate your mindset and see the extraordinary possibilities out there for change-makers like you, so you can get out there and empower your clients, your loves and the rest of the world to flourish!

www.tammyguest.com
@tammyguests

Chapter 7

Awake

Natalie Simes

*To my Dad, Mike Morrison Ryan.
And to my Mum, Janelle. Proof that love can
overflow even from broken hearts.*

We've all said it. I know I have, many times. Someone we know dies, or is diagnosed with a terminal illness, maybe not someone close, but close enough to trigger that feeling inside that reminds us that life is short. We make a promise to let go of what doesn't matter, to appreciate that life is for living. And that feeling can linger, and we might act on the call, but, eventually, we forget. We slip with ease back into everyday life, the comfort of routine and structure. It feels safe. But are we truly alive? How close do we need to be to death or illness before we wake up? A parent? A spouse? A child? Is death truly needed to catalyse life? Is illness and pain the necessary contrast to feel joy and freedom?

Is our greatest vulnerability death? Or is it choosing to live now in the face of death?

At some point, we all face the death, or an experience of illness, of someone we deeply love. In my recent experience, it's been death following a traumatic illness.

There is a kaleidoscope of emotions as you ride the wave of an illness that both rips you apart and puts you back together, repeatedly, until you think you can't take anymore.

You become acutely aware of the identities you've crafted,

and the roles you have so carefully played, can crumble. The strong one. The martyr. The rock. You are exposed. Do you double-down on the identities, or surrender to the truth of who you are?

You so often see fractures within a family when faced with an illness that will result in death. Each member of the family dealing with it in ways only they know how. Often a collection of broken hearts wanting to come together, but only knowing how to stand apart. A craving to truly feel in a world that encourages us to bury our emotions. But death can be a journey back to love. In fact, I know it can be a journey to love, but with the love comes the pain, and we need to welcome in both to experience freedom.

Anthony Simes: son, brother, uncle, friend, my brother-in-law, and gone too soon from this world. Anthony died in 2020 after an eighteen-month battle with Motor Neurone Disease. I would normally shy away from the term "battle", but a battle it was. That is, until it wasn't.

Anthony spent his life running away from who he truly was. He believed he was worthless, so he proved his worth by working himself into the ground.

He developed an illness that literally stopped him in his tracks, and he could no longer run away. He had to face himself in every way. A heartbreaking, painful, yet exquisitely beautiful journey. And not just a journey for him, a journey for our entire family.

Macy and I have just raced in to drop Anthony his morning

coffee. A quick hello, how'd you sleep, a reassuring smile from him that tells me not to worry, that I can report back to everyone that all is well in our now very uncertain world. A ritual of safe conversational questions that allows us all not to feel too deeply. To protect our hearts from facing the reality of what is speeding towards us: life without him.

Anthony was our mirror, and we had to face ourselves, too. He didn't have time for us to ask the safe questions. In the stillness, the silence and the relentlessness of the disease, he discovered who he was. Through his illness, there was a death-ing of his identities. A death-ing of the stories he'd told himself about who he needed to be in this world in order to feel love. He surrendered. Fully. Not an easy choice for someone faced with a debilitating, distressing illness. He chose to shine in the face of death. He revealed his heart. The bravest act of courage from a man who believed he was invisible.

He showed us that the true meaningful experiences in life are not what we expect—it's the love and connection felt in times of profound sadness, the shared jokes between brothers, the reassuring hand of a mother, and the realisation that truly being with someone in your full presence is what matters most. He was like a tidal wave through our family, stripping us all bare.

It's been ten nights. Ten nights thinking he won't be here when we wake. She's slept on a small, makeshift bed, barely leaving his side. I take her hand in mine. It's warm, comforting, a stark contrast to the shell of Anthony lying before me. I can see his heart pounding in his chest. His once strong, fit body, demanding to live just a little longer. But he's leaving us. I can feel him slipping away. A room often full of warmth and family, now still and quiet. But there is so much love here. Anne's steady, gleaming eyes are locked on her first-born child. She's taking in his every breath. And she won't leave him. I leave to wrap my arms around my own children, never wanting to let them go after witnessing her look at him with such heartbreaking tenderness. She stays, there for his first breath, and with him for his last. Love overflows.

Anthony gave us more than he will ever know, the gift of unconditional love and connection beyond what we'd previously experienced as a family, and a remembering to choose what really matters. He died knowing that he was loved not for what he did, or for what he could contribute, but for who he was. A gentle, kind, magnificent man who greatly impacted our family and everyone around him. He shifted our perception of illness from one of only deep suffering, to that of greater purpose.

However, those last few weeks of his life were nothing short of horrific, for Anthony, and for all of us who loved and cared for him. Yes, he was free. But the reality of his final weeks deeply affected us all. If he was our mirror, and we were now free, how could we allow ourselves to be free in the face of his suffering? In the face of Anne's suffering, having lost her son? The love was overflowing, but so was the pain. Could we honour the greater purpose of freedom?

We wanted to remain free, but our resolve was tested too soon. Before we could acknowledge and truly feel our pain, my Dad was diagnosed with Huntington's Disease not a week after Anthony's death. It was a terrifying reality, having just witnessed Anthony die from a similar illness.

The pain was too much for us all. We buried our grief. We denied our pain. We had experienced freedom through Anthony, but the weight of our grief was too much, and we were once again chained. The pain of Anthony's final weeks, combined with Dad's diagnosis, and what that meant for my family, was too much to take, and freedom was not fully realised. I chose to be safe, to bury my feelings, to become the rock I needed to be to survive. I chose to honour my identity, and deny my freedom.

We bury grief in the pockets of our soul that we don't allow ourselves to reach for. Zipped shut, padlocked, in the hope that we can close it off for eternity. The thing about grief, though; it expands when locked away and explodes from those pockets when we least expect it. We need to wear our grief like a pocket square. Slightly exposed, there when we need it, and a reminder that tears are a symbol of deep love, of connection and of our beautifully vulnerable humanness.

My Dad's journey is not an easy one. For him, for my Mum, for our whole family. It's often easier to hide our pain, to be stoic, to look for the positives in what is a tragic situation. But it's time for a softening, for us to all be vulnerable and to show our pain, to feel our pain, to fall apart. To acknowledge our grief.

My identity tells me to remain strong, to be the rock. To try to fix an unfixable situation. But, like Anthony, I can't fix this. The only thing I can do is show Dad how loved he is before he goes. To not hold back on my feelings, no matter how uncomfortable they make me.

It's ironic, or maybe not, that the end stage of Dad's illness is complete abandon of holding back. He wants us all to feel his love. In fact, he can't help but let it overflow. His tears are from laughter and happiness. His bliss is the sight of his family. Just the sight of us. No sense of obligation. Pure love and adoration for everyone before him.

We can feel the sadness for who he used to be, *and* be grateful for the person before us who just wants to love us. What a lesson. The focus can be on the illness, or the focus can be on who we can be now in the face of such heartbreak. Our choice. No removal of the pain, just a deepening of the love.

When you are living the reality that is a family member with a traumatic illness, you can deny yourself permission to celebrate. You often live in a suffocating energy, and I have no doubt it perpetuates the illness and the suffering of the entire family. The antidote is, of course, joy. It's not difficult to find moments of joy. It is difficult to allow yourself to truly feel those moments of joy. It's time to cut through the suffering, not because it's not there, but because it's time to celebrate everything. It's time to hold illness in a different energy.

How do we truly wake up when faced with a wake-up call?

What will it take to surrender? How do we take off the cloak of our identity and live freely?

To feel the love, we have to feel the pain. And then there will be freedom. Grief and pain might just be the fastest path to love, to freedom.

Just like failure is integral to success, pain is integral to love. The intensity of the pain, if you allow it, will sharpen your ability to truly show and feel love. Grieving does not mean you are a victim of your circumstances. It's a reminder that you can love deeply.

If the pain is buried, there is uncertainty and fear. Feel it. There you go. There is sadness here. But vulnerability is holding you. Be vulnerable.

My carefully curated identity tells me to turn away from vulnerability, but she's an old friend, and my instincts are telling me to lean in and listen. Her visits impart wisdom; always an offering that lingers and asks for trust. My identity will often bury these offerings, and when vulnerability knocks again, there is a remembering and a comfort. These visits show me that I should leave the door open. When she came the first time, she intended to stay. Vulnerability is the diamond of houseguests, and will reveal herself in different ways if you sit with her in the light.

It's really not just about seeing the greater purpose of illness. It's about allowing the grief and the pain, and the deep love. It's about holding it all. Feeling the intensity of the pain allows the intensity of love needed for true healing, even when that healing isn't recovery. Be vulnerable now. Be open now. Feel. Feel it all. Even when it breaks your heart.

I used to think a "good death" was passing peacefully in one's sleep. And maybe I still feel that on some level. But maybe a good death is facing yourself before you leave this world. Maybe a good death comes once you are free. Maybe a good death is an illusion. Maybe a good death is the death-ing of those parts of ourselves while we are alive that hold us back from a deep experience of life. Maybe a good death is passing having truly lived. Maybe a good death can only come when you've lived a life of deep feeling. Grief and love. An unexpected path to freedom. Excruciating pain and exquisite beauty.

Macy and I walk hand-in-hand back to the car. She holds on extra tight this morning. As we drive off, her quivering voice asks me: Is that going to happen to me? Or to Reid? My failing courage leaves me grateful in that moment that I'm driving and she can't see my face. There it is, right there. The courage and vulnerability of a child that breaks you open and forces you to feel it all. To face it all. No Mace. MND won't happen to you. Or to Reid. We have experienced the contrast, and the suffering, and there is nothing left now but love.

What if your best, honest, most loving life is nothing like you imagined? Would you have the courage to live it? I've buried myself in the safety of what I know well, saturated myself in order to avoid my true knowing. Suffocated my feelings.

I thought that through Anthony's and my Dad's suffering, we were free. But my freedom only depends on me. The missing piece is in the feeling of the emotions. You don't become the emotion. But it's essential to feel the emotions. A deepening human experience.

The journey so far has been the contrast, the cracking of the limestone to create the doors in which I can now choose to walk through. When I ask myself, what is a truer and more beautiful version of life to live, it's in the simplicity of our decision making. No logic, no explaining, just pure instinct that you alone will always know the next right thing. To trust. To listen, to let go of control and identity and to act. But importantly, to feel.

As much as I've tried, I can't bypass my feelings. The logic in me can always identify and acknowledge what's inside of me. However, my identity will rarely allow me to feel. The thought of allowing room for my feelings terrifies me. If I fall into my feelings, how do I retreat when the pain becomes too much? I must trust the freedom of the fall. For what is the result of being a swollen mess of unfelt emotion? Is feeling the path to healing? Can we feel our way out of illness? I don't have an answer. But there can be no good to come from holding it all in. It's time to let go.

Freedom is a deeply personal experience. Different for us all. If I know anything to be true, though, we must come out of the shadows of our identities to be an open heart. An open heart can feel. It can acknowledge the good and the bad and trust the perfection of it all. Maybe freedom is just being fully awake. Maybe freedom is no longer having the feeling of being caged. Maybe freedom is sending out a call to life. Being the call to life for those around you.

Freedom is the goal for me. Am I free now? Not yet. But I am committed to staying awake. And I am on the path to freedom. A constant dance between joy and sadness. An interweaving of light and dark.

Death is not my greatest vulnerability. Being awake now is my greatest vulnerability. Revealing myself in all my flaws is my greatest vulnerability. Feeling all my emotions is my greatest vulnerability. Living while I'm living is my greatest vulnerability. Let us all be vulnerable.

Thank you, Anthony, for teaching me that my greatest gift to the world is to be my true self. Thank you, Dad, for reminding me that unbridled joy and laughter is healing. Thank you both for showing me how to deeply love.

Maybe it's time to attack life with as much love and laughter as we can. If one thing is certain, it's that life will always deliver moments to break your heart, the necessary contrast so we can truly appreciate the light. All we have is right now.

Wake me up, break me open. I will be free.

About the author

Natalie Simes

Natalie Simes lives by the premise "you are not loved for what you do, but for who you are". At almost forty, she has been on a journey back to herself, determined to live a life of no regrets. After a few wake-up calls with the presence of Motor Neurone Disease and Huntington's Disease in her family, Natalie made the decision that she doesn't want to play safe anymore. As she says, 'the most vulnerable thing we can do is to be ourselves'. Natalie loves to spend time with her husband and children, as well as reading, exploring new places, and travelling all over to support her children's sporting endeavours!

Natalie, a former lawyer, hopes to create deep connections through her writing, giving others permission and support to return to, and be seen for, who they truly are.

@nataliesimeswrites
www.nataliesimes.com

Chapter 8

A timeless love story

Pina DiDonato

Dedicated to soul connections that defy time, distance and what if's

Present day. Verona. Italy.

One cannot help but get caught up in the romance of this charming medieval city. From the moment you arrive, it feels as though you have been sprinkled with a magical fairy dust, taking you away from what lies beyond the city's fortress-like walls, to a world where anything is possible.

As I stroll along the cobblestone roads, I diligently look down to avoid any missteps while simultaneously trying to capture the beauty that can be found by keeping my gaze aimed towards the sky. Every single step invokes wonder and awe. And I don't want to miss out on any of it. This city oozes love and inspires connection. And I have already fallen for it.

Set on the winding Adige River in the region of Veneto where the river meets "La Pianura Padana" is this enchanting city. Its history dates back to the first century B.C. Early in the twelfth century, Verona became an independent commune under the rule of the Scaliger family, during which the city prospered. The city fell to Venice in 1405, became part of the Austrian Empire in 1797, and finally joined the Kingdom of Italy in 1866.

Its well-preserved monuments are reminiscent of Roman, medieval and renaissance times. In fact, Verona has the greatest number of preserved Roman monuments, second only to Rome, securing its position on the UNESCO World Heritage List. It is often thought of as a smaller version of Rome, mainly because of its amphitheatre which resembles the famous Colosseum. The structure, which dominates Piazza Bra, sits stoically at the heart of the city, defying its age and captivating visitors with its magnificence, not to mention the performances that take place within it.

Verona represents a particular type of beauty—gentle, authentic and real. Powerful and strong, yet soft. Classic and timeless. A beauty that comes from within. One must look beyond the superficial to fully understand and appreciate what Verona has to offer. A beauty which is almost understated when compared to its more well-known Italian counterparts.

Verona is not the one-night stand. It is the one you genuinely fall for. It is your soulmate. The name itself has become synonymous with love.

Verona has long been considered the love capital of the world. Whether it be through clever marketing or something else, this city thrives off people's desire to believe in the magic that only love can bring.

But is it love, or the promise of love, or the illusion of love that keeps tourists flocking to Verona, the Italian city made famous by William Shakespeare's Romeo and Juliet? 'But that's just a fictional story, a tragic one at best,' I hear you say. Almost five million tourists are drawn to Verona each year, with monuments dedicated to the famous play featuring among the most popular tourist attractions. Five million people? That is the entire population of greater Melbourne, the city where I live.

William Shakespeare never visited Verona in reality, or even Italy for that matter. Yet, this is the place he chose to set the scene of one of his most famous works. How is it that he describes it so perfectly? And how years later, does this city still manage to draw in the crowds and continue to bring this love story to life?

I recall one of my favourite romantic movies set in Verona, "*Letters to Juliet*". As I retrace Sophie's (Amanda Seyfried) steps, it all begins to feel so real. First, I enter the archway which opens to reveal the courtyard dedicated to all things love: Juliet's house.

People flock to "Casa di Giulietta" to glimpse the famed balcony and to write their declarations of love on the walls, or forever lock up their love in a padlock and throw away the key. This has become a sacred space: the holder of secrets, desires and unrequited love.

Lovestruck individuals can write about their love stories or love troubles to Juliet, and their letters will be answered by Juliet's secretaries. Addressed simply to "Juliet, Verona", letters arrive from all over the world seeking advice from the Shakespearean heroine. All letters receive an answer from Juliet's secretaries. Oh, the power of love and what it can make us do in the name of it.

And then there is the obligatory photo with the bronzed

statue of Juliet. Legend has it that if you touch Juliet's breast, you will be lucky in love, or your luck with love will turn around. I have touched that breast more than once, but still, I wait in hope.

Being there is like being in the audience, an observer, watching act two, scene two unfold before your very eyes. One can just imagine Juliet, with her long silky mane of hair hanging loosely down her back, dressed in her finest blue and gold velvet gown, looking down at her one true love, while Romeo, hands raised towards the balcony, proclaims his love for her. The star-crossed lovers, declaring their desire to be together, resolve to meet the following day, to marry, despite the ongoing feud between their families, the Montagues and the Capulets.

It's a beautiful scene, one which has become a symbol of enduring love and romance.

I am brought back to reality by the shuffle of tourists trying to elbow their way through to touch Juliet's bosom. The bronze statue stands proud, ready to greet each visitor with a smile. Each touch wears out the bronze paint just that little bit more.

There's a great deal of strategy and negotiation required for your turn at touching the breast. You wait for your chance to get close. You carefully consider the plan with your fellow photographer ... 'I will go to the right boob, and you quickly take the photo from here.' It all happens so quickly, and you know you only get one shot. It's one photo—do or die. These are the sacrifices one must make in the name of love.

Channelling our protagonist, Sophie, once again, I move

back towards the courtyard entrance, making my way onto the main street. Through more archways and across to the other side of the street, I try to find the location of the restaurant where the character encounters a group of women who are Juliet's secretaries. Finding the general area, my search grinds to a halt. I look all around me. There are restaurants everywhere and I have no idea which one it could be.

As I continue to make my way through the small streets of this ancient city, I can feel the flow of energy carrying me through the city's veins, transporting me to another time. I look up at the surrounding buildings while my imagination takes a wander.

I have been to Juliet's house, but *'wherefore art thou, Romeo?'*

Drawing much less of a crowd and not permitting visitors, a now private property marks the spot of what is believed in the story to be the home of the Montague family. Meandering through the nearby streets, I can just picture the town folk walking there at night, the duels taking place in the small hidden alley ways, Romeo running fiercely to Juliet's house to declare his love.

Another short stroll leads me to the ultimate scene of this tragic love story. Because unlike most modern fairy tales, spoiler alert … this one does not end well.

It was difficult to find at first, but finally I came across Juliet's tomb, now immortalised in a stone-like museum. It's easy to get caught up in it all. Verona just does it so well. I pinch myself as a reminder that none of this is real.

As I continue my leisurely wander, I am captivated by the

buildings, the majesty of them, how solid they are. I come across the statue of Giuseppe Garibaldi in a nearby park. I am cognisant of how small I am in relation to this mammoth symbol which represents a unified Italy. In 1866, Garibaldi led an Italian army in a victory over the Austrians, acquiring Venice for the Italian Kingdom.

Built like a fortress, the ancient city is protected by impenetrable stone walls, with doors or "porte" which allow in the visitors. The walls here keep the secrets of a bygone era. They stand defiantly though so much outside them has changed. The clock towers here marked the time back then, just as they do now. Oh, if only they could speak. What tales would they share with us?

And herein lies our connection with the past. While we are only temporary visitors to this present time, these walls, these buildings, this river, these roads, have been here for centuries. And we have the privilege of feeling their embrace, albeit for a short while. These structures will remain, and they will endure, whatever comes, long after each of us has departed. Just like true love.

They have provided shelter, food, income and respite for many generations, and will continue to do so. Millions of tourists have spent time within these walls, stepping back in history, basking in its romantic energy and restoring hope and faith in love.

For love is the greatest power of all. It is something we all strive for, the ultimate goal. And Verona reminds us of this.

Whether it is romantic love or platonic love, self-love or

the love of things; love is love, and it needs no explanation or embellishment. Real love is perfect just the way it is. It has the power to transform, to heal, to overcome, to forgive, to restore and to unite. It is the connector of all things, the common denominator. The solution to many of the world's most complex problems, if only they were viewed from this lens.

And if you are fortunate enough to have or find real soul love in another, grasp it with both hands and never let it go. Run towards it and proclaim it for the world to hear, just like Romeo did to Juliet. Don't let anything stand in your way because you really do only get one chance at the ultimate prize.

But unlike Romeo, make sure you get it right because there is nothing worse than living with regret. The tragedy of this story is that our protagonists fell prey to the many influences around them which prevented them from pursuing their great love. Knowing they couldn't live apart, they chose to make the ultimate sacrifice and put an end to their lives.

Back to "*Letters to Juliet*" for a moment as Sophie responds to a letter from Clare, who shares the story of a love she let go as a much younger woman.

'What if?' she asks.

What if she had been courageous enough to pursue that great love? How different would her life have been?

And what if Shakespeare's Romeo and Juliet had made different choices? I wonder what the end of the story would have looked like then.

Do you ever wonder that about your own life? What would have happened if …

… You had turned left instead of right.

… Lingered a little longer at the traffic lights.

… Driven around for a better carpark rather than taking the first one that became available.

… Chosen to stay home instead of going out.

… Gone out instead of choosing to stay home.

I do often wonder about it …

What if …?

There are these tiny moments in life that seem insignificant in their appearance. They creep up on you, prompting for a choice to be made. Sometimes, they call for a quick reaction. These fleeting moments, where things can go either way, can have a monumental impact on what happens to you next. They can put you on an entirely different trajectory and most of the time, you can't see them coming. It isn't until you stop, reflect and join the dots that you can clearly see how you arrived exactly at the point where you find yourself right now.

These sliding door moments of one's life are those that can change the course of one's fate.

As we put one foot in front of the other, we step into what life has in store for us next. But what is it that drives those choices? Are they random, like tossing a coin? Or is there something much more mysterious at play? Are the choices we make predetermined, written in the stars or is it our destiny that guides us to make those choices?

As I look up at the stars in the clear night sky on a balmy summer's evening in the city of Verona, where one can be forgiven for romanticising about life's "what ifs", close encounters and near misses, I am most thankful for the opportunity to be right here, right now, knowing full well that every choice I have made, every step I have taken, has led me to this very moment. Present Day. Verona. Italy.

As for love, that power lives within us and can be tapped into any time we wish. Finding the ones that our love aligns with will enable it to grow exponentially. That happens as and when it is meant to. And just like Clare in the movie, it's never too late to pursue that great love. If it is truly meant to be, it will catch up with you sooner or later.

Be aware and notice the signposts, the forks in the road, the secret messages from the universe. Follow your instinct. And who knows, a little luck from Juliet's boobs may just make the world of difference. Combined with a few coins tossed into the Trevi Fountain just to be sure, what could possibly go wrong?

> *"You need only the courage to follow your heart.*
> *I don't know what a love like Juliet's feels like—a love to*
> *leave loved ones for, a love to cross oceans for—but I'd*
> *like to believe if I ever were to feel it, that I'd have the*
> *courage to seize it."*
>
> *"Letters to Juliet"* 2010

About the author

Pina DiDonato

After having spent most of her career working in a private family business, the pandemic saw Pina enter the public service where she currently works as an Executive Director responsible for communications and fundraising in one of Victoria's fastest growing public health services. Her purpose, both professionally and personally, is to make an impact wherever possible and to inspire others to do the same. Writing and philanthropy are among her passions. These have been constants throughout her life. She loves words and storytelling and the power they have to connect with an audience. She shares her insights, her experiences, and her view of the world in the hope that it can be of value to others.

Pina is a published author of *Who Switched the Lights On?*, *The Reset Switch* and *A Long Way from Home.*

@pina_didonato   www.pinadidonato.com

Chapter 9

Dating in the modern world

Suzie de Jonge

For all the tender hearts.

I never thought I would again enter the strange, somewhat bizarre and surreal world of internet dating at the wrong side of fifty-five, but a while back this is where I found myself. We all need to connect with others on some level. It is an innate part of our makeup as human beings, and that calling was making itself known to me. Yes, being single and living on your own has its huge advantages, like eating when and what you like, watching your fluffy shows on TV and being able to take up the whole bed (to name a few). But there is nothing quite like finding that person you truly want to be with and look forward to seeing who feels the same way about you.

So, how do you meet people in this era, apart from hanging out at a bar, joining a singles Meet Up Group with like-minded, like-aged people (tried that and failed miserably; I didn't know it was possible to fail at that but apparently it is!), or hoping that Mr Right might randomly find you and come knock on your front door?

I had dabbled with online dating some twenty years ago, when the internet was first born and before I met my former partner in a much more traditional and pleasant way, a blind date orchestrated by my best friend. However, it seems that things have changed mightily on the internet dating front, and well, hmm, not so much in a great way. I know I speak for a lot of other lonely hearts out there, men and women alike.

So where do you even begin on this perilous adventure? It might be easiest if I break it down into a few steps.

Step One: Find the site you connect with (or maybe several to cast the net wider). You have Bumble, RSVP, Tinder, eHarmony, Match.com, Silver Singles, Elite Singles, Spiritual Singles, Plenty of Fish, etc., to list just a few. You name it, there is a site for everyone. Warning—do your research. Some sites are not aimed at dating, but purely "hooking up" (what's with all these references to fishing!).

Step Two: Put together a profile with flattering, recent photos, a snappy catchline and try to make yourself seem vaguely interesting. Of course, most sites give you helpful "hints" on what you should and shouldn't do to make yourself "right swipe-able". (I had to do a bit of research on the "swiping" bit. Call me naïve, but there you go.) There are lots of articles on how to do this if you Google, but the bottom line is don't say all the things you *don't* want, i.e., 'don't be a d**k, no game players, leave your baggage behind, no mind games, etc.' as that can come across a tad off-putting to potential future mates, apparently.

Whilst this step may not sound that difficult, it is amazing how hard it is to describe yourself and what you are looking for in 200 characters or less. This may take some time and rejigging until you feel semi-comfortable that you are not describing yourself as:

(a) Miss Universe

(b) Bridget Jones, desperate and dateless

Somewhere in the middle is probably just right.

OK, so after hours of trying to pick the best photos you already have, or maybe putting on your glad rags and make-up and attempting a selfie (warning—don't attempt this if you are over fifty as we don't have selfie-taking in our DNA), or getting a trusted friend to take some semi-decent photos of you where you don't look too stiff and ridiculous or like a deer in the headlights and have also mashed together some sort of bio, you are ready to post your profile. This is where the "fun" (and I use that term loosely) begins. You are ready to share your profile with the worldwide web.

This can be a very vulnerable thing, people judging you, but I promise you, no more than you will judge the potential "matches" that appear in your feed or be suggested to you after you take the "compatibility test" some sites have.

This is the part where you may (if you are a woman) silently ask of the profile that comes up in front of you, *'Do you want to date a woman or your identical twin?'* Interests listed may include but are not limited to camping, fishing, motorbike riding, boating, football, World Wrestling, speed racing, climbing mountains, etc. Not that there is anything wrong with that. I am sure there are some women out there who may find that attractive, but the majority of the females I know want to meet someone who has similar interests to them, which may or may not include extreme sports.

There also appears to be a double standard with what men expect of women's profile photos, as opposed to their own. I have seen many a grumble by men that a lot of women don't look like their profiles when they meet them in person but, hey guys, this is a two-way street. Direct quote from an opening line of a profile I saw, *'Firstly, if your picture is not reasonably recent, your age or anything else is a lie then there's no need to read any further!!'* Love the two exclamation marks at the end of this sentence and, by the way, this guy's pictures were so blurry he could have been anyone!! (My two exclamation marks.)

Mr Google suggests you put photos up that are recent, are not old, are not blurry, don't include other people, don't have sunglasses in each one, etc. Most men on these sites must have missed that particular memo.

> I have seen a myriad of profile photos, and list just a sample of these below:
> - Holding one or several fish
> - One or all profile photos with sunglasses and hats on, hiding eyes and hair—or lack of.
> - The awful obligatory selfie in the bathroom (Please note: put the toilet seat down if doing this. Also … try harder)
> - Half of the person is cut off and/or blurry

- Photo is taken from so far away it is impossible to make out the person
- Photo with other men in it without pointing out which one they are (kind of like "Where's Wally?")
- Photo with another woman (hopefully not someone they are currently dating and/or married to)
- Photo with their children
- Photo of their children and not them
- Photo with their mother! I kid you not. One guy, who looked like he may have belonged to the Hells Angels, had a photo of him and his elderly mother next to his Harley. I wonder if they come as a pair ...
- Photos of their car/four-wheel drive/boat/motorbike, even earth-moving equipment (with or without them in the picture)
- Their high school and/or wedding photo
- Photos without a shirt (please put it back on) or trying to look sexy lying on their bed (it is not, just saying)
- Photos where they look grumpy and glare at the camera (or what I term the "grumpy cat face")
- Pulling crazy faces
- Dressed up in fancy dress costume

However, I'm not totally harsh. I do allow dog photos ... with or without the person in it, either is fine.

You also have your imaginative taglines, which is another first impression of a potential suitor. Again, I have listed here some direct quotes I have come across such as:

"Thought I'd give this internet dating thing a go and see what happens."

"Bush bear looking for his Goldilocks."

"Just another fat man dreaming the impossible dream on RSVP—been here ten years for zero so expecting nothing."

"I don't bite ... well, maybe sometimes."

"'This would be fun', they said."

And finally, my all-time favourite ...

"Just pick me! Or someone who looks like me! This section is way too hard and whatever I write may or may not be true."

Boom—winner, winner, chicken dinner!

Then there are the profiles where the person may list all the things they *don't* want in a future relationship, usually a dead give-away of someone who has been burnt or hurt in a past relationship. Whilst it is totally understandable and natural for some men (and I'm sure women, too) to feel this way, airing it as the first introduction to themselves on a dating profile is not really a huge turn on for a prospective mate. Rings a few alarm bells (who am I kidding—*many* alarm bells!) of painting all the human race with the same brush and/or passive aggressiveness. What is the saying? '*You attract more flies with honey*.'

There may also be mystifying acronyms included in profiles, which in my naivety again I needed to Google, such as: 420 friendly (huh?), NSA, FWB, ONS, MBA (I thought that was a degree!), poly (that one would be a "*hell* no"!). Some list their Myers-Briggs personality type: ESTJ, INFP, etc. (another thing

I had to Google). Whilst I understand these people may be intellectuals and are perhaps trying to attract their similar mate, can you just spell it out for those who may be less familiar with the world of personality tests so we don't feel quite so ill-educated?

Warning! Then you also have one of the most dangerous and beyond reproach of profiles: the catfish (more fishing references!). These are the ones who take someone's random photos off the internet and pretend to be them. They normally have unusual names like Reynaldo or Connor, and the photo will be of a silver fox, the Achilles heel for most middle-aged women, including me. They will tell you how they are humanitarians, normally an engineer or project manager of some sort, working away from their hometown of *xxx* (which, of course, is in close proximity to you). They will tell you what wonderful morals and values they have, how they want to settle down and cherish someone and, of course, my darling, it could be you (this is after one conversation). After the second conversation, this could escalate to them declaring their undying love, and the third will most likely be asking you to marry them as well as lend them money (my love) to get them out of war torn (*insert country here*) as their money is tied up in a foreign bank account, their passport has been stolen, they are in hospital, they are in jail being illegally held, etc., so they can be with you and live happily ever after. You just have to Google "catfish" and you will find many an example of some poor soul who has been fleeced out of their life savings and left with a broken heart for what they *thought* their future might have been. There is even a TV show by that same name, which exposes these fishes to their unsuspecting bait and breaks tender heart by heart in each episode.

So, if you finally find someone who you think doesn't look like a serial killer and is worth meeting, there is the obligatory "coffee date". Me, I prefer a "wine date", so if I have made a huge mistake in judgement by their profile, I can at least drown my sorrows. Many scenarios played out like this for me, as I am sure for others, again men and women alike. I would finally get up the nerve to meet someone for a "date". I would walk into the venue, see a guy sitting there on his own and think, *'hmm, that looks nothing like the guy in the picture, please don't let it be him.'* It's like a little mantra running through my mind, *'Please, God, don't let it be him, please, God, don't let it be him,'* Then said date waves at you and your stomach sinks. How old was that photo? Twenty years? In it, he had hair and didn't have a beer belly and I also thought from his profile he was taller than me (me being five foot-ish). This is the moment when you wish the ground could just open up and swallow you whole. So as not to be rude, (even though it is a challenge not to turn straight around and flee!) you sit for an obligatory coffee or drink, chit chat about nothing in particular and make an excuse to escape, such as meeting a friend or a few other especially thought-out scenarios, never to be seen again, get home and instantly unfriend or block said potential "date".

However, you may have an experience after much "swiping" to finally meet someone who seems kind of OK. The conversation may be going alright, right up until the point they start talking about their ex-partner. I kind of have a rule that if you don't know someone well, I don't think it's appropriate (or attractive) to diss your ex, take their inventory and share it with someone who you are on a date with and who you might want to see again (not so far, in my case). A person degrading and airing their obvious bitterness is not really appealing for a potential new partner. What is the phrase I am looking for? "Turn off", also another alarm bell ringer! Now, to be fair, I am only stating things how I see them from a female point of view. Believe me, women may be just as guilty of this as men.

Phew, so you finally may meet a person you like and think, '*OK, this might be something to look forward to*' and then after a meeting or two … crickets. They go quiet and drop off the grid. I didn't know, again in my naivety, that there is an actual term for this—ghosting. For me, this was the most difficult thing to deal with because you start thinking that it is about you, and you begin taking your own inventory. Thoughts like, '*What is wrong with me?*', '*What is it about me that this has happened again?*' and '*Why can't people just be honest?*'. This is the place that can be so dangerous and damaging to your self-esteem, self-confidence and self-worth. Nobody likes to be rejected. It hurts when you are already at your most vulnerable putting yourself out there.

It has taken me some time to realise it is not about me, it is always about the other person. I know, and I see my daughter fall into the same pattern, that we expect other people to treat us the way we treat them. Whilst this is an honest and transparent way to live your life, and the world would be a lot kinder place if we all did this, if you do follow this somewhat idealistic philosophy, sadly you will be hurt over and over, because that is *not* unfortunately how everyone thinks. The only actions you have control over are your own. This was the point where I needed to really look inside myself, regroup and lick my wounds. I needed to remind myself that I am unique, I am special and I am worthy. I need to love myself first, let things flow and live as though I already have that love, because I do inside myself.

I wrote a little poem and called it *"The One Who Wins My Heart"*, as a reminder to *myself* of exactly that.

*The one who wins my heart will know it is a heart worth winning.
They will want to know everything about me, and me about them.
They will value my worth, as I will honour and respect their worth.
They will realise how precious my love is and treasure it, as I will treasure their love.
They will see me for the true me, flaws and all, and still love me, as I will love them.
They will feel my tender heart's limitless capacity to love and hold it gently in their hands.
Love is not hard unless we make it so.*

So, the moral of this story, I guess, is just that. We all need connection but need to connect with ourselves first, to realise that each and every one of us deserves to be loved, and to treat each other with kindness and respect.

PostScript: Life has a funny way of unfolding and, as they say, destiny is divinely guided. Sometime after writing this piece, my former partner and I started spending time together again and unexpectedly but delightfully reunited, for which we are both very grateful and happy. It is the same but different, with the time apart letting us rediscover who we are, what is truly important to us and fall in love all over again.

This experience, however, of dipping my toes into the internet dating pool, gave me another unexpected gift, the ability to re-evaluate my own self-worth and value, something that over the years, due to many different circumstances, had become neglected and forgotten. Sometimes we all need a little reminder to give ourselves that bit of TLC and recognition that can only come from us. I hope you, dear reader, can give this gift to yourself, too. You are worthy of that.

By the way, in case you were curious, my tagline was, *"Things I have in common with Victoria Secret models ... I'm hungry."* I was just being my quirky, sassy self, and that's OK; that's who we all should be, ourselves, because you can't get that wrong. Good luck fishing!

About the author

Suzie de Jonge

Suzie de Jonge loves to share her wisdom as a speaker, author and a captivating podcast host. Her book, "*The Untangling*", illuminates the abundant possibilities that await beyond the barriers of judgment, blame, emotional baggage and limiting beliefs. Suzie vulnerably shares her personal journey with the hope of providing invaluable support to readers on their own paths of self-discovery. As a life coach, trained therapist and clinical hypnotherapist, Suzie empowers you to cultivate unconditional self-love and self-belief.

Suzie's podcast, "The Untangling" is where her gift for interviewing truly shines, filling the airwaves with an infectious sense of joy and inspiration.

www.suziedejonge.com.au

Chapter 10

The golden ticket south

Ana Asanovic

I dedicate this story to the dreamers, travellers, migrants and refugees looking for their place of safety and belonging.

2014

'Your sister lives far from the place she was born.'

It wasn't true. I was still in Serbia, in Belgrade, just across the Danube River, in a suburb called Zemun. This stunning ancient area, dating back to the first century AD, was just ten kilometres away from where I grew up.

'She said you don't live here anymore, or at least that you are meant to live somewhere far away, across the ocean.'

'Who is this person?'

Mira was my sister's friend from university and an astrology aficionado. Still getting into planets and horoscopes, she would read her friends natal charts between lectures on Immanuel Kant and Carl Jung.

I had to meet her immediately.

Restless and impatient, I got the phone number and called her over. I was living on my own, in a tiny studio apartment, walking distance from the river promenade. We were sitting on the couch, sipping espresso and looking at the chart packed with planets, angles and numbers, symbolising my life.

'You will leave two years from now, in 2016. It will take time to get the paperwork sorted.'

'Where will I go?'

'It has to be somewhere across the ocean.'

'I was thinking maybe Italy. I really love it there.'

'No, it's too close. Not anywhere in Europe. It has to be really far, and you have to cross bodies of large water. And you are definitely not going to a cold country like Canada. I see palm trees where you are. Look into Australia or possibly California.'

'Will I make it there on my own?'

'You'll love it. Just so you know, the reality of immigrating alone will hit. You'll go through a rough patch, but don't give up.'

'I wonder what that rough patch will look like?'

'It will feel difficult, but push through. Your life will change after that period, and I see you meeting your partner there. Trust me, you are not meant to find a man from here. Your partner is a foreigner, and you will meet abroad.'

There it was. Direction and confirmation. Someone said out loud what I had intuitively felt and known all along. What I've been pondering about for quite a while, but for whatever reason I needed to hear it said back to me. It was the green light I waited for, a sign. A verbal approval to put down the handbrake on my own life, and get on the road, literally.

Panic immediately started to set in.

Growing up in Serbia often means your brain is somehow wired to consider worst-case scenarios first.

What if I apply for a visa and don't get it? What does this life I am meant to be living somewhere else look like? How will I cope financially? Who is this person, my future partner, and how will I recognise him? If I don't get a visa and don't live abroad, does this mean I will be single forever?

My mind was spiralling.

July 2016

I am here, in Melbourne. It's cold, even for me, a European. On day one, I see Australia is definitely not all beaches and surf and I do need a proper winter jacket. It is beautiful and windy.

Where am I? Ah yes, Docklands. I see the water from my balcony. It's so peaceful here. My housemates are two guys in their early thirties. We all have our own rooms and bathrooms. It could have turned out way worse after I paid a hundred-dollar deposit to an unknown man from Facebook who lives in Melbourne to sublet his room while he was away.

It's clean. Thank you, universe.

I wonder how this house sharing dynamic works. Both of them are Aussies, professionals, with full-time jobs. The serious, taller one works in a bank. We can see his building from our balcony. How lucky is that, to live a five-minute walk from where you work? He is the tidy one.

The other housemate, a slightly friendlier guy, is from Perth and into social media. He often cooks Bolognese and leaves the red sauce stains all over the stove. This annoys the banker who doesn't say anything. They don't spend much time together in the living room and everyone eats their own food. I don't know if I should offer to share mine. Feels weird to eat alone every night and not to share. Sharing food is what we do.

They don't ask many questions. In an occasional hallway

chat, I tell them I am here to change careers, do another master's degree and experience life in Australia. They nod. I see they don't really want to get into a deeper conversation, even though we are all about the same age.

Polite, helpful, but distant.

I moved out a month later. As I was leaving, they were both at home, in their rooms. I wanted to say bye and thank them for everything. However, as I was rolling my luggage across the hall, neither of them came out.

I closed the door and went to Elwood.

I've always dreamed of living in a large city by the ocean. I've experienced it briefly during a trip to Barcelona and remembered thinking what a privilege of life it is to have easy access to both. All the social buzz, culture, restaurants and events at your fingertips and you could still squeeze in a swim after work or on weekends. Even the idea of just having a coffee by the beach on a Saturday morning felt like a million bucks.

This is why I said yes to a room in the leafy bayside suburb. This and the fact no one else would take me. Having been in the country only for a month, and still without any work, I wasn't an ideal candidate, at least not on paper.

Looking for a place to live did, however, give me a peek into the real life unfolding in Melbourne's inner suburbs. I stepped into the Victorian terrace houses, the workers' cottages, the overcrowded student share houses, the cold weatherboards and the fancy south of Yarra dwellings where corporate professionals lived. I saw the local corner pubs, learned to navigate tram and train lines. Admired lemon trees, manicured gardens, huge front yards. Everything had a paradise-like feel and I was so proud of myself to wait for the tram on the proper side of the street.

I looked for rooms usually in the evenings. There weren't many people on the streets at that time and most blinds were down. It was eerily quiet.

Are people sleeping this early? Why does it feel so empty? It's not even that late and the streets are dimly lit.

A friendly local explained this is what winters in Melbourne feel like and things will get better in summer. And that people prefer driving, as opposed to walking. I kept repeating to myself that I am not in Europe anymore.

My Elwood housemate, Claire, a passionate Geelong Cats fan, immediately explained the importance of footy in Melbourne. She worked in the travel industry. Travel was our common bond, our shared passion and my way onto the lease agreement.

She would come back from work around 6.00 pm and watch TV wearing multiple layers of thick, warm clothes. The ducted heating would be set to eighteen degrees. I would come home from Uni and put it on twenty. I didn't own a pair of Uggs to walk around the house in like she did and refused to buy a hot water bottle. I wondered why she wouldn't get comfortably warm in her own home. She probably wondered why I was willing to pay a huge gas bill.

The living room was her domain. The whole apartment was. She sat right in the middle of the couch, surrounded by blankets, hoodies and snacks. There was no room for me on that couch. I had to be on the side chair. Footy was often on.

Sunday was cleaning day. We took turns mopping the floors. She checked after I did my turn. My room was tiny, and we still paid rent fifty-fifty. I wasn't in a position to complain.

In those three months we lived together, she didn't have guests often. She had family and friends in Melbourne, but I never saw them. She saw them on occasional weekends for brunches or on birthdays, but nobody just dropped in for a chat.

I kept wondering why that is and if this is considered normal. I was also curious who our neighbours were and how come we didn't know them. They also didn't come by.

In those moments, I often remembered how I grew up seeing my mum and grandmother baking on Sunday mornings "for guests". We often didn't know who the guests were, but we knew someone would drop by. They didn't have to call, they were family. And of course, we had to have fresh home-made biscuits and cheese and spinach pitas in the house during the weekdays too, because 'what if someone comes over and we have no baked food to offer?' We grew up believing this was a completely unimaginable scenario for any self-respecting family and one that must be avoided at all costs.

It looks like things are a bit different here.

I am looking for work, but everyone keeps telling me most jobs are not advertised and it's all about the "hidden market". I have no networks, but I am trying. I've made a couple of friends, and keep applying for jobs, but I can't get an interview.

'What have you done in Australia?' a girl asked me as I

handed in my CV to sell shoes.

'I haven't been here long.'

She wasn't impressed with my professional experience or a master's degree from Europe. I started hiding all my education and work, made a new, simple CV and pretended I really loved customer service.

Someone who knew someone tried setting me up for a cleaning job. They rejected me, saying I need a car to do cleaning. I couldn't afford one.

Things were not looking good.

I had to find something and picked up a part-time content writing gig close to Uni. The office had no windows and the carpet smelled of mould. On the positive side, I did get to write, had somewhere to go on the days when I didn't have Uni and had some money coming in. I felt a bit better. The new job in the outer northern suburbs meant I had to leave my dream bayside area and move.

Claire advertised for a new housemate. A lovely couple came in. Passionate travellers, backpackers, just arrived in Australia. I felt bad for them, for the high price they will be paying to live in a tiny room, for the cold rooms and footy nights, the controlling cleaning, but could not bring myself to say anything.

I temporarily parted with my long Sunday walks from Elwood to Port Melbourne, collecting seashells and discovering beachfront coffee spots, and moved to Carlton.

Lygon street, the Italian heart of Melbourne, felt familiar. I could go for coffee even at 8.00 pm and that made me happy.

I people-watched for hours, locals going about their day, meeting friends or grabbing a pasta and ice-cream.

I often sat alone. Sometimes, I chatted to elderly Italians who owned the tiny family restaurants and complained how it feels difficult to culturally fit in, coming from a Mediterranean collective culture. They would smile and relate.

'You'll get used to it.'

I could see the good life all around me. It's just that I wasn't part of it. It felt like having a golden ticket to the best party in the world in your hands, but not knowing where the door is. Seeing all the fun and happiness, but looking only outside in, thorough a large window. Like standing alone in the rain, trying to somehow buzz yourself in. Hosts are not responding.

Weekends passed slowly. I soon discovered people are not usually available for a coffee unless I schedule it in weeks in advance. That felt weird. I still went southside to walk along the beach. The beach has always been my happy place. By now, I already had a favourite spot for a slice of European cake and coffee. Finding those little spots in the city made me feel like a local.

The way of life and connections between people are definitely different here. There are boundaries. Limits and unwritten rules. But I love different. I moved for my life to be different, not the same. Finally, I am able to be myself, without any expectations formed by the strong patriarchal mindset and tradition. I never cared much for tradition. I am already noticing a change—I am wearing less makeup and don't go to the shopping centres in high heels anymore. There is something liberating about walking down the streets in a city where no one knows you. I can do as much or as little as I want with my free days—and I have no one to report back to.

My phone rarely rings during the day. I talk to my old friends and family in the evenings when they wake up and I am just about to go to bed. I hear all the news, the good and the bad. My best friend's mother dies. We cry on Viber together. I can't go to the funeral.

It's my sister's birthday. First one since I left. I am picking up a card in Target. I just need an hour or two with them today. To blow candles together, to share a joke with my dad, have coffee with my mum. And I know it's not realistic. I try to hide my ruined mascara between the birthday and condolences card aisles.

Sending that birthday card was the first moment I realised my life was really here. That I have arrived. That I am physically here, in Australia. It's not an idea anymore, a dream, a possibility. When I wrote down the sender's details on the back of the red envelope, my full name under the country "*Australia*", it made it somehow official. I have an address, a home.

I left my content writing job to work at a start-up. What a change. I loved the start-up vibe, the people and all the brunches and Brunswick coffees we did together. But they ran out of funding, and I had to leave.

What now?

Weeks went by without any call backs for a job interview. I wondered if this was the difficult period Mira was talking about. A period where you are hopeful about the future, but life is far from how you would like it to be. A time where nothing is certain and possible roads to happiness are not fully visible yet.

My friends are giving me unsolicited advice online. They keep telling me what Australia is like, even though they've never lived abroad and keep wondering how come I can't find work. They ask me if I've seen a koala already and if all my dreams have come true. If I have settled in. I feel too weak to keep explaining. I don't want to go into what it means to have part-time working rights, to try to work and study, to do things alone most of the time while figuring out how the whole system works. How increasingly disconnected I am starting to feel from them, while I haven't formed strong friendships here yet. On some days, I don't even pick up their calls. The distance between us is more than just physical. I realise I need to fight this thing with a clear head. But I do miss them. There is so much of Melbourne life they would love. I see how their lives could be better here, too. I see the possibilities in their fields, and my heart breaks for the years we've all lost, hoping things will change back home.

A dream keeps repeating. In this vision, I am in Belgrade for a visit, and trying to come back to Australia, but I can't. I am stuck at the border, and I lose my chance of getting out. I wake up, my heart is racing, and for the first couple of minutes I don't know where I am. Then I realise, I am in Melbourne. I am still here. Nothing is ruined yet, everything is fine, there is a chance that things might still work out.

I know what this is. I know where it's coming from, but I don't know how to make it go away. Before moving, I often felt like I was in a prison cell, punished for a crime I never committed. That I was part of collective, tragic and disastrous destiny and that I don't have any control over my life. That my life is a string of random events unfolding between tall, grey, claustrophobic walls and I have no idea what is on the other side, even though I am desperately trying to see. That I am living only a black and white version of my life. Now that I am finally on the other side of the wall, that prison cell still haunts me.

I installed Tinder and Bumble. If someone told me I would be on two dating apps, I would have said a firm no and that I was too serious, mature and romantic to go on dating apps. That there wouldn't be anyone there for me.

Spending weekends alone or sometimes with my housemates wasn't the best option either. By this time, I was brave enough to have coffees alone, walk into a restaurant and ask for a table for one, but wasn't going alone to pubs or clubbing. That's where the date would come in.

Most men talked about investment properties like I knew what it meant. While they talked finance, I was wondering when my rent was due and how much money I even had left. I could feel my body posture changing and my mood shifting. Some of them were worth another date, others ghosted me and some would never even meet in person. Few could relate on a deeper level.

They talked about childhoods on the farm and asked me about mine. Initially, I mentioned the ten-year-long civil war, how my family fled to Canada when I was only eleven, and then came back, how I was only seventeen when Serbia was bombed and how I can't play cards anymore because that is all we did in hiding. How I avoid going to any military or air shows because something creeps under my skin at the sound of fighter jets. How I come from a destroyed country with no prospect of recovery. How this new life has to work because I don't know what I would do if it doesn't.

But that wasn't sexy talk, and it was a real first-date mood killer. So, I talked about my travels through Europe, safaris in Kenya, how much I loved Italy and how nothing beats staying with the locals. I was trying to keep it light. I focused on my other passions—food, writing, my travel blog, my friends both in Serbia and the new ones I am trying to find in Melbourne. But mostly, I let them speak. This online catalogue of easily accessible dates opened the doors to the diversity of people, thinking, backgrounds, life and experiences I'd never dreamed of before. I am trying all the different cuisines of the world. I realise I really love Indian food, even though all my life I assumed otherwise. Mexican is fantastic, too, and the Lebanese is heaven. I know what a Parma is, and I had the Pavlova for Christmas. I am a citizen of the world and loving it.

I found something to do. Actually, I got two casual jobs, in hospitality and events. The barista I worked with was a lawyer. Another one was an accountant. We are all migrants. While we served the customers, I often wondered if they had any idea of the lives their wait staff were leading and the dreams they were working towards.

My master's in strategic communications is almost done.

At least there I have nothing to worry about. Except finding a professional job. I keep sending resumes and swiping on the apps.

I pause on one photo. He is looking at a distance, wearing a navy coat. A family member took the photo. I can see the backyard and part of the kitchen. I can tell he is tall, with a light brown beard hiding ginger undertones and deep, dark green eyes. He holds a proud posture, facial features resembling the ones on my high school philosophy books. I need to message him first. That is how the app works.

'Are you Greek?'

About the author

Ana Asanovic

Ana Asanovic is an empath, storyteller and a captivating public speaker. She enjoys working on projects that make a real impact, driven by her creative and inquisitive nature. As a migrant and refugee, she openly shares her personal experiences and reflections, including stories of career changes and the power of following your intuition. Ana has more than 15 years of professional work experience across communications, languages and the written word. As a lifelong learner, Ana is both a mentor and mentee, eager to learn from others and connect over shared food and cultural experiences. In her day job, she's a Strategic Communications Manager and a passionate advocate for sharing diverse stories of resilience and triumph.

@anabythebeach

Chapter 11

Happily ever after: a work in progress

Anita Carr

I felt like I was in slow motion, like life was happening around me but through this dense, murky fog. I could see movement and shadows, yet everything felt so out of reach. I was existing, but I wasn't living.

I had no control over what was happening. I was just there. Suspended. Numb.

I knew I wasn't happy. I knew I didn't feel like me. I knew this wasn't the life I was meant to be living. You're told the story of meeting a man, falling in love, getting married, having kids and living *happily ever after*. We assume that *happily ever after* just happens. But what if you're still waiting for it to arrive? What if it never comes? Was there any evidence that it even existed? And what is it anyway?

Happily. Ever. After. After what? After the expectations of giving our everything to everybody. Meeting everyone else's needs except our own. After we get left at the end of every day with nothing. Day after day.

We weren't warned about the feeling of being so … *nothing*.

We often paint a picture of our life for the outside world to see, because that's how it *appears* to be, even in our own mind. How we want it to be. But it's like we trick ourselves into believing that it's true. We push down the feelings that persistently creep up. The questions that keep rising to the surface … *Is this it? What if there's more?*

Until recent times, we rarely talked about what happens behind closed doors, during the so called *happily ever after* part of our story. All the life-altering things that take place during this time, whether they feel significant or not, shouldn't be neatly packaged up into a box with a bow and placed on a shelf, labelled:

'It's just part of it.'

'Everyone goes through this.'

'We all have tough times.'

'It's not that bad.'

'It could be worse.'

'This is life.'

'I'll be fine.'

The between bits of *happily ever after* and *death do us part*, that are so goddam hard, no one seems to want to talk about. Because then we could be seen as negative. Ungrateful. Selfish. A bad mother. A bad wife. So, we suck it up. We take the hits, and we don't complain. But they add up over time. Even if we aren't consciously keeping score. Our body does. Our subconscious does. Our nervous system does. And one day, it all adds up and it equals, '*I've had enough. This isn't enough. I want more. I want so much more.*'

I'm going to tell you what happened between my *happily ever after* and *death do us part,* or in my case, *till divorce do us part*. The significant events that occurred and the moments that felt insignificant at the time, that all weaved together and how they led me out of this tangled web I felt so bound by.

After I got married at twenty-eight, everything moved quickly—house, baby one, baby two, baby three. Six years after my *happily ever after* was supposed to begin, I was happily ever lost. I'd always been the good girl. The people pleaser. I made everything joyous. I made sure I created joy for everyone around me. Everyone I loved. Sometimes I felt some of that joy I had created, sometimes I didn't. But to the naked eye, I was totally living my *happily ever after*. In reality, I felt alone. Unsatisfied. Undervalued. Unloved. Weak. Squashed. Nothing.

I was unhappy to my core. I knew this life was not what I had envisioned. Yet, I had all the things that I wanted. Well, the things I thought I wanted. The things I was told I should want by family, friends, movies, books, songs and society in general. The story we are fed to want. I knew my relationship wasn't what I had expected it to be. I was lonely. Traditional gender roles naturally evolved. The woman stays home, raises the children and carries the mental load, while the man works and provides for the family. It would be unreasonable to want anything more, wouldn't it? I knew I had to get out. I was so unhappy, drowning in the everyday of three children under five. I just didn't quite know how. Though it seemed the universe did.

Seven years after my *happily ever after* was supposed to begin, my marriage took a hit when illness struck. It was sudden and it was brutal. I remember thinking, '*If he pulls through, this is our second chance. Maybe this is what we need. Maybe this will change everything?'* I honestly believed it would. And it did change everything, just not in the way I had imagined.

Alone, for three months with three young children to navigate life. Initially, I was terrified of that prospect. The whole situation was unbearably overwhelming, and it literally brought me to my knees. But as time went on, I got stronger. I was doing it! I was doing it on my own. I started to feel more *me*. I felt stronger. I felt capable. I felt lighter. I felt free. When it was time for life to go back to normal, I started having panic attacks. I didn't want things to go back to the way they were before. I could see that's exactly what was going to happen. There wasn't the miraculous change, the second chance I had hoped for. I knew this reaction wasn't normal. I felt like a monster. I felt guilt. I felt shame.

I tried to save my marriage for another year. I didn't want to fail. But the *me* that had started to emerge during those months on my own quickly slipped away. I was spiralling out of control in all areas of my life. I wasn't coping. I felt so trapped. I wanted to escape. Little did I know that these feelings, all that I was experiencing, were about to make so much more sense.

My eldest son was in Year Two at the time and was struggling with his learning. I decided to investigate and discovered he had Inattentive ADHD. I knew little about ADHD. I knew the stereotypical symptoms: hyperactivity, trouble focusing, behavioural issues. But my boy wasn't any of those things. I spent days and nights researching, trying to understand what my beautiful boy was going through so I could help him. I didn't want him to struggle. I wanted him to thrive.

While researching Inattentive ADHD, which I had never even heard of before, I opened the book to my whole entire life. There, right in front of me, were the list of things I had felt as long as I could remember. I'd always felt slightly different. I'd always felt things deeply. I felt my brain worked differently to others. The wrong way. But I did everything I could to make it look like my brain worked the right way. I had been masking my ADHD symptoms for thirty-seven years. No wonder I felt so exhausted and overwhelmed.

ADHD isn't just hyperactivity. It can be part of it, but it's not all of it. Inattentive ADHD is more of a daydreaming brain. You zone out. You get bored easily by things that don't interest you. The world in your head is so much more interesting than the real world. Whether you have Inattentive, Hyperactive or Combined ADHD, your body and brain get accustomed to living in fight-or-flight mode. Your cortisol levels are constantly through the roof. This is why any sign of stress can push us over the edge. Our emotions are constantly dysregulated. This is why I wasn't coping. The stress of everything that had happened, and what I was currently experiencing, was too much for my nervous system. I was on the verge of a breakdown.

The thing with ADHD in women is that a lot of the symptoms are stereotypical traits associated with being a woman. Anxious. Chatty. Forgetful. Scatty. Emotional.

No wonder it never got picked up! Whenever any concerns had been raised in the past, the reason was always, you're a woman. You just need to relax.

Everything suddenly became clear. I was having an

awakening and a shutdown simultaneously. There was relief that my life now made sense, but then there was anger and hurt that I had lived thirty-seven years of my life struggling internally and not knowing why. Thinking it was normal. Thinking that this is what everybody felt, and they got by, so why couldn't I? Shame and guilt raised their ugly heads yet again.

Around this time, I knew my marriage was most definitely over. I was gaining clarity in all areas of my life. It was now apparent that the *happily ever after* I was told about, but had no idea what that meant or entailed, was never coming. It was a farce. It was created to keep me inside that box with a bow we put on the shelf. To make me believe that this was all I ever wanted, and I should be grateful for it. That there was nothing more I should want.

The separation took a long time. Longer than it should have. There was COVID. There was the guilt. There was shame. Eighteen months after officially separating, I finally started to find some peace living on my own. To live my life the way I wanted to live it. To understand my ADHD and work with it rather than against it.

I gave myself permission to start living on my terms. Because, for the first time, I felt I could do that. Yes, there were circumstances, expectations, pressures, societal views etc., that kept me feeling trapped in that box, but I realised I allowed myself to be kept there. At times it felt like all sides were welded shut. But in reality, they also had hinges I could push or pull open, as much or as little as I wanted. I just had to believe that

I could. That I was able to.

Having the time and space to *see* and experience a new perspective, plus learning of my ADHD, made the box I felt I would never get out of completely disintegrate. I began to really understand myself. Listen to myself. Know myself. Accept myself. And by doing this, the fog lifted.

There was a faint path. A yellow brick road, if you will. I knew I had to follow it. I looked back on the path I had already walked, and I could see the good times and the bad. The love and the loss. The joy and the pain. The sunshine and the rain. Where I made wrong choices. Where I could have done better. Where I needed to do better. Where I had to forgive myself. But I couldn't really regret any of it. Because it all taught me something. It all led me here. And while I knew there would be plenty of bumps on the road ahead, and some of the bumps were a hell of a lot bigger than I had anticipated, I knew there was so much more down that yellow brick road for me. I just had to be brave, take the first step, and let the gravity of all that was out there for me, pull me closer. I had felt the pull for a really long time, and instead of resisting it anymore, I let it take me.

I think *happily ever after* does exist. It's just not the end of the story. It's a work in progress. Ever changing. And it sure doesn't begin once you get married! It begins when you decide you aren't where you are meant to be. When you know you want more for yourself. When you know you deserve more. When you realise that what you are told isn't necessarily what you *know*. You *know* what you want. You *know* you can go get it. That you *will* find a way. As women, we just have to fight for it. We have to go against what we have been told for so long.

Yes, it can feel scary or even impossible. But if you could read your *happily ever after* right now, what would you hope it would say? What do you *know* it should say?

I know mine would say ... And she lived *happily ever after,* committed to being the most authentic version of herself, living her life, with the people she loved, doing things she loved that brought her joy. Learning and growing as she goes. Being brave at every step, no matter how uncomfortable it made her feel. And *knowing* she was capable of getting everything she truly wanted. That she was worthy of having everything she truly wanted. And she would. She knew she would.

Happily. Ever. After.

Pleasure or contentment. Sense of trust and confidence. At all times. Always. The time following. From this on.

About the author

Anita Carr

Anita Carr is a writer, ADHD advocate and enabler of joy! She is fiercely passionate about living authentically, joyously and unapologetically while embracing our diversities. She shares her stories vulnerably on social media and in her articles published on media outlets online. Anita lives in Perth, Western Australia with her three beautiful children, who inspire everything she does.

www.anitacarr.com.au
@anita_carr

Final thoughts

In conclusion, *Unity* is not merely a collection of stories; it's an urgent call to action, an ember that ignites the flames of connection and compassion within you. Its purpose is to plant the seed of belonging deep within your heart, reminding you that vulnerability, authenticity and connection are the cornerstones of profound personal change. But now, it's your turn to step into the spotlight of your own story.

As you've journeyed through the pages of this book, have you felt the resonance of your own experiences within the tales shared? Have you sensed the threads of your life interweaving with the lives of these women, forging a tapestry that binds us all together? Take a moment to ponder: What unique stories lie within you, waiting to be uncovered and shared? How can your vulnerability and authenticity lead the way to transformation in your own life?

Unity has been your guide, your source of inspiration and your confidant on this path. But now it's time to let your own stories shine. Consider this not an ending, but a glorious beginning, a chapter where you join a profound, transformative journey. Ask yourself: How can your experiences empower and inspire others? What brave steps can you take to share your story with the world, making your voice heard in a powerful way?

Unity has given you the tools and the courage to embrace your own narratives, to uncover the liberating potential of your shared existence. It stands as a reservoir of strength and a source of inspiration as you navigate the complexities of life. But remember, you are not alone in this endeavour.

As you turn the final page, envision the path ahead as a road illuminated by the stories that have come before you. The collective power of *Unity* will create a brighter, more interconnected world.

www.ingramcontent.com/pod-product-compliance
Lightning Source LLC
Chambersburg PA
CBHW020321010526
44107CB00054B/1931